Scottish Fold Cats

Scottish Fold Cat Owners Manual.

Scottish Fold Cat care, personality, grooming, health and feeding all included.

by

Clifford Worthington

CW00550296

Table of Contents

Introduction

The History of the Domestic Cat and the birth of the Scottish Fold

Cats have been part of human civilization for centuries and long before the Scottish Fold was even first born cats had become an important member of the family. Before we discuss the origins of the Scottish Fold in particular, you may be interested to know how the domestic cat first came in to being.

Cats were first domesticated thousands of years ago in both Africa and China. The Chinese, along with Iran and Afghanistan, began to domesticate cats somewhere between 2000 BC and AD400. However, it was the Egyptians who would eventually introduce feline domestication to the entire world. Domestication first took place in Egypt descending from the African Wild Cat. This wild feline proved its worth by providing vital pest control to protect grain stores from vermin and it was slowly moved in to the home. The Egyptians were quick to study their new feline friends and the cat became a sacred animal, often regarded as a deity in its own right.

Cat owners revered their pets and when they died they would shave off their eyebrows in displays of mourning. The cats would be embalmed and mummified; they would then be taken to temples such as the Great Temple of Bast, which was built in tribute to the cat god Bubastis. By around 900BC the Egyptians took their new domestic deities to Italy and the population of the cat as a pet grew as the Roman Empire expanded. In the 10th Century they arrived in England.

Once again the cats were used for practical reasons and became reliable methods of pest control, especially at sea, which led to them being taken to the New World. However, they still remained rare and it was not until the 17th century that shorthaired cats gained popularity in the US and in the 19th century longhaired cats were first imported.

Up until the 19th century all cats were crossbreeds. Reproduction occurred through accidental meetings and natural selection. However, humans started breeding pedigrees and artificially created more than one hundred cat breeds. Therefore, although now referred to as 'pedigrees' all cats are essentially, to some degree, mongrels.

Throughout the next century, new breeds were established and celebrated by pet owners and cat shows alike. To reach the origins of the Scottish Fold you have to fast forward around a century to 1961. It was then that the first Scottish Fold was found and then later documented in 1966 with the Governing Council of the Cat Fancy. A litter of farm kittens had been born in Coupar Angus, in the Tayside region, just northwest of Dundee in Scotland. The litter had one anomaly; a white kitten had developed small ears that folded over towards her face. When the kitten had matured she gave birth to two more kittens, one of which possessed this same physical trait. A neighbor of the farmer and cat fancier, William Ross, had been paying close attention to this unusual cat and decided to try and produce a new breed using one of the kittens. The kitten was bred with a British Shorthair and from then on the Scottish Fold was officially born.

What was to follow would be a controversial story, as more research in to the breed found their propensity towards genetic mutations a drawback to the existence of the breed and one that questioned the very ethics of its breeding. The UK, Australia and New Zealand have officially denounced the breed as cruel whereas further research in the US has found that combining the breed with British and American shorthairs has been found to decrease the risk of disease.

However, despite this division in the cat fanciers and genetic community, as a pet the Scottish Fold gained a reputation as a loveable and loyal cat that has made them perfect for the cat owners of our times. They are easy going and never violent, they are not mischievous but still playful and adapt to changing situations well. We will go in to more detail as to the breed's tumultuous back-story and genetics later, but it does not prevent this cat from becoming an extremely popular pet.

Chapter 1: The Scottish Fold – Early Breeding and Genetics

1. The story begins

After William Ross had started the process of breeding the Scottish Fold, he brought in the purebred British shorthairs to standardize the breed and its particular type. The early 1960s saw Pat Turner, cat breeder and geneticist start her work on the Scottish Fold. She found that the gene that causes the characteristic folded ears was a dominant one. This means that as long as one of the breeding cats has the fold, the litter will be born with the fold also, this made it very easy for breeders!

In 1971, the first Scottish Fold was born in America after William Ross and his wife Mary shipped some of their kittens to Neil Todd PhD, a geneticist living in Massachusetts. After a few rounds of breeding by himself and some fellow breeders the Scottish Fold became recognized by the ACA in 1973, this was followed by recognition from the ACFA and the CFA in 1974. By 1974 the Cat Fanciers' Association of the United States gave the breed its championship status. In the meantime, work had begun to develop the long-haired breed and this was achieved by 1987-88 when the variation of the shorthair was recognized by TICA.

In 1984 the Cat Association of Britain followed suit, when the shorthair Scottish Fold was officially recognized as a championship breed. However, despite its popularity in the US the breed has never been fully supported in its native country. This is generally believed to be because of the genetic make up of the breed, which is prone to hereditary skeletal defects and faces reluctance from breeders and fanciers alike, which will be discussed later. Despite this, Scotland is still recognized as the true home of the Scottish Fold and William and Mary Ross as the original breeders.

Throughout the years the difficulties of rearing the Scottish Fold Cat became apparent. The same gene that causes the fold in their ears can also result in a number of cartilage and skeletal abnormalities. We will explain the problems that can occur with these specific genes later on but it remains to say that since they are descendent from farm cats the Scottish Fold is a fairly sturdy and ever loyal breed.

2. Not welcome home

Scottish Folds have long been a favorite among cat fanciers in the US and regularly appear in the best cat shows in the country. However, the breed is not so revered in its country of origin. This is because of the health problems that are associated with the breed and caused by the same genetics that causes their ears to fold.

It was quickly discovered that breeding two cats with folded ears was creating genetic disorders and William Ross took the measure to breed with British short hairs to stop this from happening. However, even with these measures taken, there were increasing numbers of crippling deformity on the breed's limbs and susceptibility to infections, mites and in worst cases, deafness. In 1971 the Governing Council of the Cat Fancy withdrew Scottish Fold registrations and the breed has struggled to regain any footing since this happened.

In the US the breed has been welcomed with open arms. The initial problems that led to the breeds deregistration in Great Britain seem to have been bred out. This is due to breeding with American and British shorthairs. We will discuss in a bit more detail later about what you should check when buying a Scottish Fold, but any good breeder knows that two cats with folds should not be bred together. It is this inbreeding that caused the majority of the genetic problems and it is important that they are not able to return.

3. To fold or not to fold?

For a breed to be completely disregarded in its country of origin it must raise questions as to the ethical issues surrounding the breed.

In the 1970s, a research study in to the Scottish Folds found that the reason the breed had the folding forward ears was because they had he genetic disease Osteochondrodysplasia (OCD), we will go in to more detail about the disease and how to spot it a bit later. The findings of the research found that the disease was not just affecting cats with homozygous genes, i.e. cats with both parents who have folded over ears, but those who have heterozygous genes (one with the fold and one without).

As has already been mentioned, not all Scottish Folds are born with the folded over ears, this in itself is an indicator that they are not affected by OCD to the same degree. So why continue breeding cats with folded ears? Well, this is where the controversy lies. Criticisms towards breeders of Scottish Folds claim that the desire to breed folded-ear cats is for pure aesthetics, that some people just like the way it looks.

So what can you do as a pet owner? Well, there is no 100% guarantee that your Scottish Fold will suffer greatly from OCD if he/she has the folded over ears. But they certainly will carry the disease and suffer to some extent. Later on we will discuss how is best to check for the disease in kittens before you buy or adopt. We will also discuss neutering or spaying your cat. This will ensure that the disease is not transferred through further generations of cats.

The general consensus in the US claims that there is not enough information yet to completely cease breeding of the Scottish Fold. But research from Great Britain, Australia and New Zealand has concluded that this is the only option to ensure cats do no suffer for purely human desires to have a cat with folded over ears.

Either way, the Scottish Fold remains a popular with cat owners the world over and the whole point of this guide is to give you all the information so you know what to expect from this controversial yet loveable breed.

Chapter 2: Scottish Fold Appearance

1. General appearance

If there's one overriding word that encompasses the Scottish Fold stature, it is 'round.' Due to the folding over ears and large round eyes it is often remarked that the Scottish Fold's appearance resembles that of an owl. The same gene that creates their folded ears also attributes itself to a very distinctive appearance.

Face: They have a round face with a shortened snout and rounded whisker pads, sometimes leading to what appears to be a very smiley face! Their eyes are large and round while their nose is short and goes out in to a gradual curve.

Body: Their fully rounded body has plenty of padding and their tail is shorter and thicker than most breeds. Their short, thick legs lead in to strong stocky feet that are designed to carry this unusual frame.

Size: They are a small to medium sized cat and generally weigh up to 9 -12lbs/4-6kg when fully grown.

2. The folded ears

The Scottish Fold's name came from its most defining physical feature, the folded ears. However, their ears are not always folded; many cats develop no fold at all, these are often referred to as 'Straights', in fact this can happen just as often as cats with folds.

Not only this but their ears are definitely not folded in the same way from one cat to the next. Originally Scottish Folds had just one fold in their ears but due to inter species breeding this has now become more varied. Some still have just one fold bent forward from about halfway up the ear, while others posses a 'double fold' or even a triple fold. The triple folds are sought after for show cats. However, they are all still very much Scottish Fold breeds in every other sense of the word no matter how many folds are in those ears.

3. The cat of a thousand colors

One of the many advantages of choosing a Scottish Fold as a breed is the variety of coat types and colours you can opt for. Firstly, you will have the choice between longhair or shorthair, they were bred from both Persians and Short-haired breeds and so either way you will find a vey dense coat. In the longhaired Scottish Fold, the length and distribution produces a coat, which is fullest and longest around the ruff and britches. The coat then drapes softly without the long heaviness of a Persian cat's coat. The longhaired cat will also encompass the toe tufts and ear tufts.

Next you will have the choice of a wide selection of colors, from wonderful blues to the eclectic tortoiseshell varieties. Colors from many sources were combined and allowed in the development of the Scottish Fold. Not all of these are officially recognized for show cats but the fall list can be found online.

4. "The Buddha Position"

Another common feature of the breed is their stance. Many owners remark that their Scottish Fold like to sit upright on the sofa with their back upright and their paws resting on their belly. This is sometimes seen in other breeds but usually only when grooming, however the Scottish Fold like to sit this way when relaxing, giving the appearance they're sitting with you watch the TV!

Although it is a very unusual position for cats to naturally hold, this is due to their general physique and it is a comfortable way for the Scottish Fold to relax. They have also been known to sleep lying on their backs in an almost doglike fashion.

5. General Information about the Scottish Fold Cat

Weight in the Male
>12 lbs/ 6 Kg

Weight in the Female
8-10 lbs/ 4-5 Kg

Eye Color
Copper, Gold, Green, Blue, Brown

Life Span
9-13 years

Attention Demand
Moderate

Length of Fur
Short or long

Texture of Coat
Smooth and dense

Color
Various

Allergenic Property
Moderate

Grooming Need
Low

Prevalence of the Breed
Rare

Chapter 3: Scottish Folds As Pets

1. What are Scottish Fold cats like as pets?

If you're in the market for an aloof character in your cat, then you should probably stay away from the Scottish Fold. One of the things that make them such a popular cat is their ability to form strong bonds with their owners.

They do not enjoy being left alone for long periods of time and when you are home they will often seek you out for some attention. They are not overly playful or energetic, which is why they make perfect apartment cats. They do, however, really need that attention from their owners and are prone to erratic behavior if left on their own for too long. If you work long hours then it could be advisable to get a companion for your Scottish Fold or even get a pair as kittens.

There are a number of factors to consider when owning any cat, so I've addressed some of the questions you may be having when considering your new Scottish Fold Cat.

Are they good around children? In truth, no cats appreciate being pulled and prodded so there is a certain amount of acclimatizing young children to cats rather than the other way around. We will talk about this in greater detail later. But any pet is a great addition to a family and children that have grown up with pets are more likely to have a good sense of empathy towards animals and people and have strong communication skills. To be good with children a cat needs to be sociable, relaxed and patient. So this means the Scottish Fold is a perfect cat to have if you have children. They will form a strong bond with your children and as long as they are handled gently will enjoy spending time with them.

What about allergies? Unfortunately there are no fully hypoallergenic cats but there are some that produce less of the allergens that cause reactions in humans. The Scottish Fold is no exception to this rule. Obviously the degree of molting depends on their coat length too but generally speaking they are not the most hypoallergenic breed to own.

How are they around other pets? It can be difficult to introduce any new cat to existing cats in your household but there are techniques we will explore later in the book, which will make the introductions a little easier. When it comes to dogs the Scottish Fold is happy to be around any cat-friendly dog. As with all pet introductions, they should be done in a controlled environment and we will go in to detail about this later on in the book.

2. The personality of the Scottish Fold

The Scottish Fold is one laid-back, loyal kitty. Here we give you three of the breed's defining personality traits to show you just what makes this breed so loveable.

3. The cool customer

If you're looking for an easy-going cat, the Scottish Fold is the perfect option. They are not overly playful or excitable, which is a blessing if they are ever placed in unfamiliar surroundings. You may find that when taking them to the vet, they do not panic or scratch half as much as some other breeds. They tend not to be perturbed or put out and can get on easily with other pets and children.

This trait makes them a very easy cat to handle and one that you can trust won't destroy your curtains while you are at work. This is not to say they are not playful, however. They can chase yarn as well as any other kitty, but the difference with the Scottish Fold is they won't cross the line from playful in to boisterous. The only drawback is that it may be more difficult to encourage them to play as they get older as their natural inclination tells them to curl up on the sofa. But it will only take a little encouragement and as long as you play with them no less than three times a week they will keep up their general mobility.

Their tendency to relax also means they are not very vocal. It is a rare occurrence indeed for a Scottish Fold to meow, moan or protest in any way, which makes for a good nights sleep for their owners!

4. That loving feeling

Scottish Folds are a perfect combination of laid back yet affectionate. They may not demand too much from you, but they will always seek you out and welcome your company. Scottish Fold owners find they are followed around the house and often called upon form some lap time later in the evening.

One of the reasons they love your lap and being around you could be because they love warmth. You will usually see them basking in some sunlight or just curling up in front of the heater. They may even creep into a warm blanket and just laze around there sometimes. So, it is quite natural for this breed to seek warmth from the bodies of their owners. This is why they are usually very attached to their owners. Scottish Fold owners often talk about the manner in which their pets follow them around the house. They will walk right behind you and follow you from one room to another.

This need for warmth and affection makes the Scottish Fold a perfect lap cat. If your pet finds a vacant space on your lap, be sure that he will leap right up and make himself comfortable. Scottish Folds are not affectionate with just one particular person like most cat breeds. They will be just as cuddly with any other member of your family. Sometimes, they also get friendly with complete strangers.

The Scottish Fold is particularly fond of human company. They do seek a lot of attention and can get easily upset if you ignore them. It is quite surprising how different this breed is from the others. They will seldom leave your company and will always be right beside you. If not on your lap, your Scottish Fold will be curled up around your feet or will gently rub itself against your legs to make sure that you are not going anywhere.

The Scottish Fold also loves to participate in all your household chores with you. If you are folding your laundry, your Scottish Fold will be perched at the exact same spot where you are most likely to put away your clothes. If you are tidying up in your bedroom, everywhere you turn your Scottish Fold is likely to be there waiting to see what you'll do next.

The amount of love that these cats have to give is exceptional. They will, most definitely, share your bed if you let them. They will curl up beside your feet or neck and may even make you their mattress when they are in the mood. When you decide to get a Scottish Fold, make sure you understand that you and your cat are inseparable.

Obviously this attachment to their owners means they do not like to be left alone. As we have discussed before, if you are away from home a lot, the Scottish Fold is not the cat for you. You may find they become agitated and display signs of distress when they are left all day, so companions are essential. If you work long hours and do not want two cats, it is best to look elsewhere. But if you want feline friend who is curious, affectionate and loyal to their owners, the Scottish Fold is the cat for you.

5. Got the smarts

As characteristic of many of the quieter, more subdued breeds, Scottish Folds are highly intelligent cats. Later we will discuss how you can test your Scottish Fold's intelligence but averagely speaking you may have a little feline Einstein on your hands. They are constantly inquisitive and like to know what is going on in their house. This intelligence attributes itself to their adaptable nature and easy temperament; it's not easy to flummox a smart kitty!

They love to keep an eye on things around the house. For this reason, they will choose the highest vantage point to look down from. If they are not cuddled up in your lap. Unlike most cats, you will rarely find the Scottish Fold hiding under sofas and tables. This is true even when there are strangers in the house.

Scottish Fold cats adapt themselves very easily to their surroundings as well. They are extremely sensitive and are able to get along with just about anyone. They will also make themselves comfortable in the household without much effort from your end. It is easy to put a Scottish Fold into a routine because of its high levels of intelligence and adaptability.

Although it would be great if we could completely predict what your Scottish Fold will be like please bear in mind that there can be anomalies and every cat is different. Each breed does have its common characteristics but there is always a certain element of potluck with any pet purchase or adoption. To help break this down below there are some ratings so you can check at a glance if the Scottish Fold will fit in with your life:

Personality trait	Rating
Affection towards the owner	5/5
Adaptability	5/5
Intelligence	5/5
Independence	2/5
Playfulness	3/5
Compatibility with children	5/5
Compatibility with other cats	4/5
Compatibility with dogs	4/5

6. The benefits of owning a cat

Owning any cat has been proven to bring with it a huge amount of health benefits. Strangely enough their purring especially is at just the right frequency to lower stress, lower your blood pressure, help cure infections, decrease the signs of dyspnea and heal muscles and bones. Cat owners are also 40% less likely to suffer from heart attacks.

Cat owners tend to be more relaxed and according to a study held in Switzerland, the effects of a cat on their owner are similar to that of someone with a romantic partner. This doesn't mean to say you should substitute a human partner for a cat (well, not always anyway!) but the point is cats provide a loving and calming atmosphere to come home to.

They may also help bring in a new romantic interest if you are a man; according to a study held in Britain, 82% of women are more attracted to men who own a cat. But remember, cats are for life, not just until you meet a partner!

Ultimately we have cats as pets because they provide amazing companionship; all the health benefits are simply bonuses. Also, we must note that there is a clear correlation to good health and cat owners, rather than necessarily a cause. Meaning people who chose to own cats are just more than likely relaxed and laid back people who do not wish to take care of a high-maintenance and attention seeking pet. Therefore they are less prone to stress related illnesses, regardless of them owning a cat or not. But we can all agree that it certainly cannot hurt to bring a cat in to your life and Scottish Folds especially are up there with the best when it comes to having a fully devoted and affectionate cat.

Chapter 4: Preparing For Your Scottish Fold

1. Are you prepared for a cat?

Owning a cat can be a relaxing and trouble-free experience. Cats are less demanding than dogs and require much less in terms of exercise and grooming. However, there are still lots of things to do to make sure your cat is happy. Especially your Scottish Fold, they're not always easy to please!

Everyone living in the house must be prepared for the arrival of the cat. Whoever you are sharing your house with must be informed about the changes that might be made to accommodate the cat in your home. They must be prepared to be patient with the cat to give it ample time to adjust to the new surroundings that it is in. Only when your new pet is comfortable in the house will everyone be allowed to handle it and play with it. With a cat that is as friendly as the Scottish Fold, you will be surprised at how easy this phase is.

It is also important to ensure that every member in the family has a checklist of 'Dos and Don'ts' with respect to the new pet. You must establish rules like keeping doors and windows closed, keeping chemicals locked away and also putting food away to make sure that the cat is safe. One very important instruction is to check washers and dryers before turning them on!

So, to begin, when you are buying or adopting a Scottish Fold cat, there are some things that you must consider:

- **Life Span-** The ideal lifespan of a Scottish Fold cat should be between 9-13 years. Check with your Scottish Fold cat breeder about the history of your cat to understand the history of the kitten's parents and their life span.

- **Temperament of the Cat-** Although Scottish Folds are known to be of a very gentle temperament, you must enquire about his social skills. He will most probably take after his parents and his behavior will be similar to theirs.

- **Older Cat or Kitten:** This is a question that you will definitely face when you are looking at buying a new cat. Scottish Fold cat rescue homes and adoption centers will help you find a suitable adult cat. However, if you are looking at raising a cat, you may want to get yourself a kitten instead.

- **Cost-** A Scottish Fold can cost up to $1,200. However, this higher price is attributed to cats with a pedigree certificate. Of course, if you decide to adopt a Scottish Fold cat, you will get your cat for a much reduced price and sometimes perhaps free.

- **Does your cat need a friend?** Research shows that cats that grow up in pairs are the happiest. So, if you want to get your cat a companion, you can ask your breeder for the most suitable option.

- **How pet friendly is your home?** A Scottish Fold is the perfect apartment cat. So even if you live in an apartment, it will not really matter. However, if there are any restrictions with respect to keeping pets in your apartment, you must be aware of it. In addition to that you must make sure that you also have access to pet stores and vets in the area that you live in. If you feel that your home is inconvenient for your pet, you might want to rethink the option of owning a cat.

- **Your Lifestyle-** If you feel like your Scottish Fold will not have enough company while he is at home, do not even think of purchasing a cat. Scottish Folds crave attention and can have several health complications if they are not given ample love and affection.

Once all these issues have been sorted, you can prepare your home for your new Scottish Fold.

2. Preparing your home for your new Scottish Fold

From the day that your cat has arrived in your home, do not expect it to wander all over the house. It is natural for the cat to pick one spot in the house and stay there till it is well acquainted with the surroundings. Cats may hide for a few days; it is only natural as they may not be very comfortable with the change in environment.

It is a good idea to choose this room for him. When you bring your pet home, set him down in a dedicated room called the 'Bonding Room'. Do not disturb the cat. Just shut the door on your way out and let the cat be. This is a very important step because you will be giving your cat a 'territory' to gain control over. Leaving him alone will make sure that he is not too anxious to explore the new area.

You can make your pet feel more welcome in the room by placing some water and food in the room. You might have to leave a litter tray in the room as well. But make sure you keep the litter tray as far away from the food tray as possible. By nature cats are extremely clean creatures and will not appreciate eating close to the litter tray. If you want the room to be more comforting for your kitty, you can even get special cat perfumes like the "Feliway diffuser" to keep the cat calm and happy. With these special perfumes, your cat will be able to relax even in a completely strange setting. They are all available at popular pet stores and even with your vet.

It is important to keep some bedding for the cat. Once the cat gets accustomed to a soft cushion, blanket or a cat bed, it will never sleep elsewhere. To attract a cat to this sleeping place, you can leave some catnip toys or other toys. A cat like the Scottish Fold will most often prefer to collect items that it loves to play with and bring it to the bedding area. Allow him to do this, as he will feel more comfortable with things of his own preference.

Leave the carrier in the bonding room. You can even look for cat tunnels and place them in the room. Creating a space for a new cat to hide in is a great idea. Of course, the cat will only hide in places that he feels really safe in. You cannot control that but it is good to leave them enough options.

Although the Scottish Fold is very comfortable and in fact thrives off being around human beings, the time that any cat takes to adjust to a new place varies. There are several habits and behavior patterns that your cat may display. There is no need to be alarmed or even disappointed with them. All you need to make sure is that you are prepared to give your new pet time to get used to you. The most common observation with cats is the time that they take to get out of their bonding room.

Some cats stay confined to this bonding room for several days. It does not mean that your cat dislikes you. Once your cat feels secure, it will be out. Unlike dogs, there is no way you can persuade your cat to come out of hiding.

There are several things that the cat needs to get accustomed to before he decides to venture out into other spaces in the house. The smells and sounds around him are the first things that he must get accustomed to. There are several sounds that are new for him. Your voice, the sound of the telephone, the sound of your car starting in the driveway and all other sounds that seem quite ordinary to us are a big deal for your new Scottish Fold.

There are several smells, like the smell of your furniture and carpeting that he must become familiar with. Why, he must also get used to your smell. It is through these pieces of information that the cat analyses how safe the environment is from him.

To make sure that you also allow them to get used to the house, try to avoid the following:
- Loudspeakers while watching movies
- Vacuuming the bonding room
- Hosting loud and noisy parties
- Inviting all your friends and families to see your new pet
- Constantly trying to pick up the cat and pet it

When your cat is ready, he will come to you without you even trying. Especially with the Scottish Fold you can be certain that he will crave for your touch and warmth. Ideally, it takes between 3- 7 days for a cat to get accustomed to the space. However, there are simple things that you can do to make the bonding experience easier for you and your new Scottish Fold.

Prior to bringing your Scottish Fold home for the first time you may want to ensure your house is completely kitty-proof. A good idea is to go through this checklist and make sure everything is taken care of before your cat arrives.

Ornaments: Cats like to explore and it's impossible to stop a Scottish Fold when they are being nosy. This wanderlust can lead to accidents so make sure your precious ornaments and other breakables are out of reach of your cat.

Doors and windows: The first thing to establish when buying or adopting a cat is weather you are going to have a house cat or an outdoors cat. If your cat will be staying indoors make sure all doors and windows are secure.

Electric cables and appliances: Cats and kittens especially will chew or scratch at most things so to prevent any nasty shocks ensure cables are out of reach.

Kitchen: There are many hazards in the kitchen for a cat. These include hobs and hotplates, sharp utensils, plastic bags and white goods. Always make sure your cat stays away from harmful areas.

Open fire: If you have an open fire in your home it is essential you put up a fireguard prior to bringing a cat in to your home.

Other pets: If you have a dog it is best to set up a separate area for your cat straight away so boundaries are established and your other pets do not feel threatened in any way. This will be explored in more detail later on in the book.

Chapter 5: The Costs of Owning a Scottish Fold Cat

When adopting any cat it can seem like a fairly cheap option for owning a pet. But the on-going costs can be significant so ensure you are financially able to care for your Scottish Fold. Here we breakdown all the costs that cat ownership will entail:

1. One-off costs

The Cat

$90- $1200/ £50- £1000

Depending upon the breeder and whether he/she gives you a pedigree certificate or not, costs can vary drastically. We will explore further the fluctuation and what you are paying for if you go pedigree.

Council Registration

$40/ £25

In some countries it is a legal requirement to register your cat with the council. This is necessary to obtain required licenses for your cat.

Neutering/spaying

 $100-200 / £60-120

Although some breeders may take care of this, you may have to decide and pay for the procedure yourself. The costs vary from one vet to another.

Microchipping

$50/ £30

In some countries, microchipping is mandatory. This is a good option to ensure that your cat, if lost, can be reunited with you at the earliest.

Vaccinations

$50-$70/ £20-£50

Never ignore or neglect vaccinations. In the first year, your cat will need about 3 vaccines.

Cat Carriers

$30-$50/ £15-£30

You will definitely need a cat carrier to make trips to the vet or travel with your beloved Scottish Fold.

Scratching Post

$100 approx/ £60 approx

If you want to safeguard your home from havoc, make sure you get your kitty a scratch post. The costs may be higher depending upon the type of post you choose.

Cat Toys

$30/ £15 for basics

There are so many toys available on the market that you can certainly not put a price on this. However, for a basic selection, you will pay about $30. You must not neglect cat toys as they are necessary for good exercise for your cat.

2. Ongoing Costs

Food

$10/ £6 per week

There are various brands that you get on the market. The price of the cat food will depend entirely upon what you choose to feed your cat.

Litter

$8/ £10 per week

This is just an approximation. The costs may vary as per the type of litter.

Worming Medications

$2.50/ £1.50 per week

These topical medicines need to be re-applied regularly.

Veterinary checks

$70/ £40 per annum

This is the cost for routine checkups only. It does not account for unexpected accidents or illnesses.

Pet Sitter

$10- 25/ £5-10 per day

Insurance

$20-60/ £7-36

The best option with insurance is to do your research, different companies can provide insurance quotes based on your cat breed and age so it is worth weighing up the options and making sure you are willing to make the investment.

Chapter 6: Buying or Adopting Your Scottish Fold Cat

1. Buy or adopt?

There are many advantages to both buying and adopting but ultimately it depends on you and your situation as to which option you choose. It is worth noting that Scottish Folds can be highly sought after in the US and also quite rare, so when seeking your Scottish Fold with their distinctive ears, you may find buying is your only option. In which case there is almost certainly going to be a waiting list.

Whenever you are planning to bring home a Scottish Fold Kitten on sale, make sure you talk to your breeder about the personality of the cat that you are looking for. They will be able to find the right Scottish Fold Kitten that will suit your requirements. When a breeder recommends a certain kitten, they will keep in mind the temperament and the attitude of the parent cats to determine the personality of the kitten. Since these breeders also stay with these cats from the time they are born, they watch and understand how they behave with people.

When you buy a cat or kitten the likelihood is you will be going to a breeder or to a private seller whose cat has had a litter. To find reputable Scottish Fold breeders in the UK, check the Breed Council Secretary and in the US check the CFA in the US. The International Scottish Fold Association will also provide details of breeders and is recognized by the CFA as a good resource for information. When going to a breeder you can see where the cat has come from and request details on their veterinary history and the cat's mother. When buying it is important that you ask to see the mother to ensure the seller is reputable and it can personally be of benefit so you can roughly see how big your cat will get.

Buying can be expensive depending on the breeder and whether you are going pedigree or not. Cross breed Scottish Folds will start at roughly around $120/£80 but essentially it is up to the seller's discretion and no matter pedigree or not if it is a particularly cute litter a seller may up the price. Pedigrees will start at around $500/£500 and can go up to around $3,600/£2,000 if the cat is from a good family, i.e. if they are award-winning pedigrees.

2. Adopting a Scottish Fold

Since Scottish Folds are of a premium, it is fairly unlikely a pure breed will come up for adoption. However mongrels will certainly be available. Adopting any cat can be an extremely rewarding and transformative experience for the cat and owner alike. Everywhere is in need of people to adopt unwanted, stray or poorly treated cats but there is a lot to consider before committing to an adopted cat. It is best to check that you are prepared to provide the following if you are considering adoption:

- Necessary care in case of reported abuse
- Constant care to help him adapt
- The necessary nutrition if he has health issues.
- Vet assistance if he is ill or old
- A separate room or enclosure to protect him and other pets at home

Obviously if a cat is in an animal shelter the likelihood of having all the information on their exact breed and background in terms of genetics will be difficult. When a cat has been given up by previous owners or abandoned you may be inheriting some significant health issues that the previous owners were unable to care for. This means extra financial and practical considerations will have to be made. Often any cats that have been poorly treated will be naturally distrusting of humans and this can manifest itself in many different ways. They may be aggressive, prone to spraying, nervous or suffer from health problems as a consequence. An older cat from a volatile background may not be a suitable option for houses with children as they may be aggressive towards unpredictable movements. Often you will have to pay an adoption fee to cover the costs of the animal shelter so do not expect to adopt a cat for free. However, in terms of helping animals in need this is an extremely worthwhile way of owning a cat. If you are confident of being able to provide all of the above, adoption is the noblest thing that you can do for your pet. Give him a loving home where he will be able to learn to live a life of dignity and happiness.

3. What to look for when buying your Scottish Fold

Once you have decided that the Scottish Fold best suits you and your home environment the fun part starts and you can begin looking for your cat. If you choose to adopt then you may not be able to check everything, such as seeing their mother and gaining their veterinary history, but the animal shelter should be able to provide you with as much information as they can.

Try not to be entirely swayed by a cute face, which is definitely easier said than done, especially with the Scottish Fold! But do try observing their behavior and getting a feel for their personality. With the questions posed in Chapter 2 in your mind ensure you are picking a cat that will suit your home and lifestyle. This is particularly important if you have other pets. If choosing from a litter, take note of how they interact with their siblings; are they submissive? Are they playful? Are they aggressive?

If adopting or buying a kitten, make sure they are at the correct age. They should be between at least 9 to 12 weeks old, a little older than 12 weeks is ideal. If you adopt a kitten any younger than this you are not allowing them the vital time with their mother and siblings. This time is essential in their development and helps them learn important skills such as litter training and other behaviors. After 12 weeks the kitten also has a much stronger immune system and will stand less chance of getting ill when you take them out of their birth home.

Once you have spotted the Scottish Fold kitten or cat that you like, spend a little time with them. Have a play and sit with them. This will help both of you get used to one another and you will get a better sense of their temperament. Do not be instantly put off if they bite or scratch you, if you've never had a cat before you may have approached them in a way they do not like or they could have just been playing. As with a dog, you can tell if a cat is inherently aggressive in the way they interact with you. When approaching your cat hold out your fist first and encourage them to get a scent for you and nudge it, this is a friendly greeting. Picking up the cat is fine but they may not be overly enthusiastic about it; this is perfectly normal and is by no means an indication of what she will be like as a pet. There will be plenty of opportunities to get your kitten used to being around you and your family.

If possible ask to see the mother and request to see their veterinary records. Seeing the mother gives you an idea of the environment the kitten was born in to and if you get the chance to see the mother with your kittens this will allow you to gain more impressions of how she deals with other cats. Some breeders keep the mother separate from her kittens, this could be for a number of reasons and is not unusual, however, still ask to see the mother. The veterinary records will allow you to keep track of their vaccinations and will be of use to your own vet.

4. How to look at a cat when buying

If you think you've found 'the one' there are a few things you should check for before making your purchase or signing the adoption papers.

With Scottish Folds there are a few things you should be wary of. Make sure that both parents of your Scottish Fold do not have folded ears, this combination can cause many genetic disturbances such as the most common problem, Osteochondrodysplasia. It is also important you check their tail; degenerative joint diseases can be displayed in the tail so run your finger along the bottom of the tail and at about half way bend it slightly downwards. If the flexibility is good, your kitten is okay; it is very important that you are gentle when doing this, as tails are a sensitive part of a cat's body. Lastly, just watch the kitten walk and ensure it is not unusually unsteady on it's feet, this can be a sign of underlying joint problems too.

Next, check their eyes and ears for notable signs of infection. The eyes should be bright, open and free of any discharge. Their ears should be clear without any black discharge and should not smell bad. The nose should also be clear and not runny and you should also look out for constant sneezing.

Take a note of the cat's breathing and respiratory system. Breathing should be smooth and regular without wheezing and coughing. Place your hand on their chest and take an estimate of their breaths per minute; this should ordinarily be around 20 to 30. To do this count how many breaths they take in a 15 second period and times by 4. Panting or over labored breathing could be a sign that something is wrong (unless they have just been playing).

It is important that you also check their bottom. The anus should be clean and in no way inflamed. If a cat has worms you may notice small tapeworms around the hair in the area and this should be treated straight away. You should also check for signs of diarrhea, both on the cat and in the litter tray.

Next you will need to check their coat for any ticks or lice. Run your hands through the coat and inspect the belly, armpit and around the neck, these are key nesting grounds for fleas and lice. Also check for any bare patches of fur; these could be the result of ringworm or other diseases.

If you suspect there may be a problem request that your vet look over the cat or kitten before you buy or adopt. Any reputable breeder or animal shelter should be happy to oblige.

5. How much should you pay?

Since Scottish Folds are a rare breed of cat you can expect to pay at least $500 in the US and £500 in the UK. Obviously if the kitten is from a champion lineage you can expect to pay even more as we have previously discussed. You will also find that if your kitten does not possess the fold in their ears it will be a little cheaper than those that do.

If you would like a pedigree breed there is a lot to be careful of when considering a purchase. It is vital that you go to a reputable breeder and are able to see the mother when you visit. Often you will have to put down a deposit of around 10-20% to secure your kitten and in some cases, put on a waiting list. If you are buying to potentially show the cat it is of vital importance that the cat is registered. There is a list with each breed having been given its own code including all coat colors officially recognized. The GCCF in the UK and the ACFA in the USA offer comprehensive lists of recognized breeds, which are eligible for shows, but The Scottish Fold is not one of them in the UK.

Not all pedigree cats are of show quality so you can still buy pedigrees without the elevated price tag. Within a litter there is much more chance of the cats being just pet cats rather than show cats but they will still be much more expensive than normal adoption.

As with any expensive purchase it is important you do your research to make sure your breeder is offering you a price in line with the market. The ACFA would be able to recommend breeders and having their stamp of approval is an assurance that you are paying a correct price. In addition to your kitten you should also receive their 'papers'. This includes their pedigree certificate, injection certificate and their registration slip. The pedigree certificate usually displays the past 4 generations and any information of show winners within the family. If a kitten has a mother of grandmother who has won a major show this may push up the price. If you are paying the high price for a pedigree cat it is well within your rights to demand one of these certificates. The injection certificate is just the same as with any other cat and outlines the vaccinations that your cat has had. The registration slip is what sets the quality cats apart from normal pet cats. If you are buying a pedigree for a pet there is no need to have this slip, but if you plan to show your cat this slip is proof of recognition from the pedigree governing body. If you plan to show the cat and the breeder refuses to provide the slip this should set alarm bells ringing. Any quality cat that is entered in to a show reflects very well on the breeder so a reputable breeder would not just supply the certificate but insist on it.

You may also have a microchip certificate if the price includes a microchip; this is worth the extra money if you plan on letting your cat outside. Not only does the microchip assist if your cat gets lost but also quality Scottish Fold cats are of a high premium and would be prey to criminals looking to make money in the illegal trade.

Chapter 7: Outdoor Cat or Indoor Cat?

For those living in flats or apartments, having a pet can pose a slight dilemma. Very few indoor spaces provide your pet with ample space to play around and exercise. This can often lead to people opting out of owning a pet, as it is often considered 'cruel' to keep them inside. However, there are a number of cat breeds that do not need as much stimulation as others and actually prefer indoor living. Luckily one of these includes the Scottish Fold. They enjoy staying inside and being with their owners.

1. Myths about indoor cats

Despite the temperament there are a number of considerations that go through the mind of any potential indoor cat owners. Luckily, these are often just myths:

Lack of exercise can lead to weight issues: It is not mandatory for a cat to go outdoors to get the exercise that it requires; you can easily prompt them to stay active even indoors. A good option is to purchase a cat tree for them to climb. Scottish Folds are often regarded as fairly playful cats and should find ample stimulation here, not to mention giving them plenty of scratching space. However, if you do not have the space for a cat tree, there are plenty of toys that will provoke your cat in to exercise. A spool of thread, a toy mouse, a ball of yarn or a paper box can all become a great playing tool for your pet. The most important thing with an indoor cat is the environment that it lives in. If you can make your home comfortable for the cat to run around and play in, you need not worry about taking him outdoors for some exercise.

It is not possible to domesticate a cat to stay indoors: This is not true, especially with the breeds we have mentioned before. These breeds choose to stay indoors, they get the sunshine, sights and sounds from a windowsill. You can also walk cats using a harness. This way you don't have to worry about getting the cat the amount of outdoor time that it requires. Most cat breeders might recommend an enclosure to keep your cat safe outdoors too, this can be useful if you do have a garden.

The pet might urinate and dirty the house: Cats, as a species, are very easy to toilet train; in fact, their mother usually takes care of this from when they are born. Sometimes you may notice they urinate outside the box, but if your cat is otherwise healthy, this is usually a sign that the litter box is full, it is inaccessible or the litter has changed and they do not like it. If your cat continues to litter outside the box even after you have addressed all these points, make sure you consult a veterinarian.

The cat might scratch and ruin the furniture: Unfortunately there is an element of truth to this myth. Any cat likes to keep their claws sharp and so it is natural for them to scratch hard surfaces. If your cat is not trained or a scratching post has not been purchased you could potentially expect your furniture to be ruined in just a few days. In the next coming chapters we will outline the best way to combat the behavior, but regardless of whether your cat is indoor or outdoor this is just comes hand in hand with cat ownership.

It is unhygienic to have a cat at home: Cats usually tend to walk on high surfaces like kitchen cabinets and shelves. In case you do not find this comfortable or hygienic, you can train the cat to only occupy certain spaces. However, cats are extremely clean creatures and due to their own diligent self-cleaning do not carry the high levels of bacteria that dogs tend to. Also, if your cat is an indoor cat the likelihood of them bringing in outside germs is greatly reduced. So what seems like a drawback to having an indoor cat is actually a major bonus.

Pregnant women get infected by cats: Many people believe that women who are pregnant can contract a disease called Toxoplasmosis if they come in contact with cat feces by accident. In actual fact, this disease is most often caused by the consumption of uncooked meat. However, in order to be safe, pregnant women should always wear gloves while cleaning litter boxes. The cat is not a threat to the well being of the pregnant woman and can be allowed to stay indoors without the danger of any infection.

2. Why is it better to have an indoor cat?

There are several reasons why an indoor cat is a more convenient option, in fact Scottish Folds are quite happy indoors and require little strenuous exercise. Here are a few things that you might want to consider if you are thinking of choosing an outdoor cat over an indoor cat.

Traffic is one of the biggest reasons to keep a cat indoors. If you live close to a high way or reside on a street that is relatively busy, you might want to consider a cat that will spend most of its time indoors. Even the smallest accident can be fatal for your cat or might result in serious injuries.

Cats that roam outdoors are most susceptible to infections from other cats. Feline Immunodeficiency Virus or Feline Leukemia is quite common in cats that roam outside. These diseases are usually transmitted from one cat to another. If you allow your cat to roam freely, there are also several possibilities of cat fights with other stray cats in the neighborhood. This leads to injuries and abscesses that make it hard for both the owner and the cat. Not only do these injuries cause a lot of pain to your pet, they will also cost you several hundreds of dollars to take care of and treat. If your cat has not been properly vaccinated, then it runs the risk of several other diseases that are prevalent in the outdoors.

Parasites are common issues faced by cats. It is very easy for fleas to attack your cat if it is usually strolling freely in the outdoors. Some fleas may also carry diseases that are deadly for the cat as well as its owners. Some ticks also have the potential to paralyze the cat permanently or even kill it if not treated correctly. Fungi like ringworm can also infect your cat, this can be passed on from cats to their owner quite easily. Although it is not a deadly disease, ringworm usually recurs in cats and is not easy to treat or get rid of.

If your cat is outdoors often, there are several other dangers that it will encounter. Domesticated cats are usually not able to defend themselves against animals like dogs, opossums and snakes and will either end up being seriously injured or even die due to these attacks. If your cat ventures into wrong territories by mistake, it becomes vulnerable to these attacks. Cats are also susceptible to attacks from people as well.

A cat that is allowed to roam outdoors is most likely to get lost. There is also the threat of potential theft, the chances of which increase if you have a pedigree cat. So it is best that you either opt for a cat that stays indoors or at least ensure that it has a collar with information to identify it. According to statistics, close to 10% of cats rescued in animal shelters are not reclaimed by their owners.

Skin cancer is also a problem with most cats, especially those with fine hair and no undercoat. In the case of cats with dark fur, the threat of skin cancer due to excessive exposure to the sun is more prevalent. If you live in a country or a part of the world where skin cancer is highly prevalent, you must consider protecting your cat from exposure to sunlight.

You might also face several social problems when you allow your cat to roam outside. It is possible that your cat litters your neighbor's garden or simply ruins a beautiful flowerbed. In either case, you might find yourself quarrelling endlessly with your neighbor. It is impossible to locate and control a cat that is used to the outdoors.

Contrary to traditional belief, a cat that stays indoors is known to be healthier and happier. Considering all the threats that you are protecting it from, there is no reason why you should not believe this. Research proves that cats that are allowed to stay indoors also have a longer life than cats that are allowed to roam freely.

Although there are some cat owners who are not particularly fond of keeping the cat indoors. This is the only way to ensure that your cat gets the benefits of staying outdoors while being protected from the dangers that are prevalent.

Chapter 8: Getting To Know Your Scottish Fold Cat

1. The first few days

Bringing a new cat in to your home can be a very exciting and rewarding experience. As they explore, get to know their surroundings and yourself you will start to notice their little nuances and gradually their personality will come through. However, in the first couple of days your new Scottish Fold may be stressed, a little listless and confused. It is important that in this time you give your new addition to the family some space.

You must never reach for the cat or try to cuddle in the beginning. If your cat is not nervous by nature, he may just come to you on his own. What you should do, however, is visit the cat regularly. Walk into the bonding room, sit on the floor or a low seated chair for a while and call out to him in a voice that is soothing. It is okay for you to walk in and out of the house as long as you leave him alone for a couple of hours in between. Even if it takes several sessions to get your cat to even greet you, don't lose your patience.

In case there are children in your family, make sure that they visit the cat only when they are accompanied by an adult. At least in the initial days, this is mandatory. The reason to take this precaution is that children might get excited at the sight of the cat. If they startle the cat, he might just become anxious and even scratch or harm the child. So, never let children near the cat without proper supervision.

The Scottish Fold loves attention. If you do not give your Scottish Fold the time he/she requires, it is quite likely for them to end up feeling depressed. You do not have to play with them, necessarily, just make your presence felt in the room. If there are several people living in your house, take turns to visit the cat. Just hang around in the room and allow the cat to get used to you.

You will know that your cat is getting used to the bonding room by his behavior. He will not continue to hide from you. With Scottish Fold cats, you will know that they are ready for you, as they will want to leave their scent on you. They will affectionately rub themselves against your legs. However, if you try to touch them, they may resist it in the beginning. To lure your cat towards you, you can make use of toys. There is no better toy than a shoe lace or a string. All you have to do is run it along the floor and your cat will not be able to resist the temptation to pounce on it. This game is the best ice breaker between you and your cat. Once your cat gets used to you and the surroundings, be prepared for him to fuss over you and play with you all the time.

There are some special cases when you, as an owner, have a larger responsibility towards your pet. If you have a dog, a resident cat or even a child in your house, the steps you take to introduce the cat will be different. As mentioned before, the Scottish Fold has a certain pecking order that it prefers. Another unique case is when you adopt an adult Scottish Fold cat. Here are some simple measures that you can take if you are wondering how you can make your Scottish Fold feel more secure and comfortable.

2. Noticing the signs

Cats are not like dogs and when they are happy, sad, frustrated or anxious they may not let you know so blatantly. Each cat breed acts in different ways and essentially the best thing you can do as an owner is observe your cat's behavior and this will help you understand their nature. However, there are some key telltale signs that will help you read your cat's mood.

The tail is a helpful indicator of a cat's mood. If their tail is straight up they are content and happy. When it is moving from side-to-side they may be feeling tense. When it is fluffed up they are on the defensive and this is usually combined with the hair on their backs fluffing up also.

Purring is usually a good sign and one that shows your cat is relaxed and happy. However sometimes purring can be a sign of anxiety. In this case you should be able to tell the difference from a normal purr, it is usually slightly more high-pitched.

If your cat is looking for attention from you they will make it very obvious, usually coming over to you and brushing against your legs. Scottish Folds will follow you around the house anyway, not necessarily looking for attention but feed their inquisitive mind and just wanting to be close to their owner. However, if you notice that they are being particularly clingy and purring it could mean they are either hungry or they wish to be stroked. When a cat wants you to stroke its back it will lie down and raise its hind legs. When it rolls on to its back it is usually looking for a scratch on the belly or wanting some playtime.

When your cat is anxious there are many signs it will display. Do not worry if these last for a short spell, it could be anything that has caused a slight change of mood in your cat. But if the below persist there may be something causing it which you can change.

- Tense body
- Dilated pupils
- Aggression
- Spraying (territory marking) indoors
- Nervous grooming
- Soiling indoors
- Chewing wool (this usually only occurs with Siamese or Burmese cats)

If you think your cat may be anxious you may be able to do something to help. Essentially anxiety usually occurs when there are changes in your cat's environment. If you notice these signs try and pinpoint when the behavior started to occur and what you can do to rectify the situation. You may have moved the furniture in their favorite spot or they could have lost a companion. The important thing is they are given space and time to relax and with time they should get back to normal. The change in mood may also be due to another cat encroaching on their territory. If this is the case your cat should relax once it has reestablished its own space or if you can identify the culprit chase it from your garden when it arrives.

3. What makes a cat happy?

Despite the famous Scottish Fold attachment to their owners, all cats no matter the breed, need a sanctuary where they can relax on their own. This means an area to sleep, stretch, wander and stare till their heart's content. More often than not your cat will find this area on it's own and you will not need to do too much. It is natural for the cat to pick one spot in the house and stay there till it is well acquainted with the surroundings. Cats may also hide for a few days, this is only natural as they may not be very comfortable with the change in environment. Just try to not disturb the area too often and too drastically. If you do need to move around their area they may not be too happy about it but cats are more adaptable than they are often given credit for and they will find a new space to call their own if they need to.

If you have other pets you may wish to dictate this area more than usual and pick a space in the house for them to avoid any conflict. When you bring your Scottish Fold cat home, set her down in a dedicated room. Do not disturb the cat and just shut the door on your way out and let the cat be. This is a very important step because you will be giving your cat a 'territory' to gain control over. Leaving her alone will make sure that she is not too anxious to explore the new area.

You can make your pet feel more welcome in the room by placing some water and food in the room. You might have to leave a litter tray in the room as well. But make sure you keep the litter tray as far away from the food tray as possible. If you want the room to be more comforting for your new cat, you can even get special cat perfumes that you plug in to the wall to keep your cat calm and happy. With these special perfumes, your cat will be able to relax even in a completely strange setting. They are all available at popular pet stores and even with your vet.

It is important to keep some bedding for your cat too. Once your cat gets accustomed to a soft cushion, blanket or a cat bed, it will never sleep elsewhere. To attract your cat to this sleeping place, you can leave some catnip toys or other toys in it. Some cats will bring their favorite toys or even take some dry food to their bed with them. This is perfectly normal behavior exhibited when you have other animals in the house.

Leave the carrier in the room you have chosen for your cat. You can even look for cat tunnels or trees and place them in the room too. Creating a space for a new cat to hide in is a great idea. You cannot control that but it is good to leave her enough options. Some cats will stay confined to this room for several days. It does not mean that your cat dislikes you. Once your cat feels secure, it will be out. Unlike dogs, there is no way you can persuade your cat to come out of hiding.

Cats are also very fussy about hygiene and if they feel unclean or neglected they will not be very happy. If you do not clean the litter box regularly, you will notice peculiar behavior patterns like littering in other places inside the house. Some cats will also not eat well if the litter box hygiene is not maintained appropriately. Always examine the litter box and ensure that the litter is replaced on a regular basis.

As we have already discussed, the most important thing for Scottish Folds is company. They like to be with you when you are home and do not like being left alone. This is an extremely common trait in the breed.

4. Playing with your cat

Playing with kittens is an important part of their development. It teaches them cognitive skills and gives them exercise to improve their agility. They will be extremely playful in the first few months and after about 6 months this will start to gradually drop off. The best way to keep your cat playful in to old age is to get another cat, this way there is a constant source of socialization and play.

However, even if you have more than one cat it is always important to dedicate some playing time to them cat in order to keep them sociable, although this may reduce to just once every other day and for a shorter period when they get older. Scottish Folds are not the most playful of breeds; they are never boisterous and tend not to get too over-excited. But it is still vital that they get some chance to play and improve their agility.

As far as toys go there are many household objects, which provide plenty of entertainment for your cats. A Ping-Pong ball provides endless entertainment for all cats, giving them the opportunities to chase and pounce. For kittens yarn gives them something to chew on and they enjoy chasing it also. A fun game is to take a cardboard tube and drop things, either a ball or toy mouse down it while your cat waits a the bottom; this gives them pouncing practice.

Many store-bought toys include catnip and are usually found stuffed in toy mice or in balls; this makes them irresistible to most cats. The effect of catnip can be short lived but reactions can vary. Some cats rub against it; others roll on their backs and stare in to space while some run around the room seemingly playing with an invisible friend. Some cats get very possessive over their catnip toys and may turn aggressive after use. If your cat becomes aggressive perhaps substitute for honeysuckle or valerian products.

5. Introducing your Scottish Fold to other pets

Scottish Folds are notoriously adaptable and few owners report any problems of integrating their Scottish Fold with any other pets. However, it is important that initial meetings are controlled as your current pets may not be so adaptable and any new animal arriving on the scene can be cause for concern.

It is often remarked by cat owners that it is easier to introduce a new cat to a dog rather than to existing cats in your home. This obviously depends on the dog, if your dog is already used to cats there should be very few problems and likewise if your cat is adopted and used to being around dogs you will find once they have got to know one another they will settle in to their new arrangement. But with the following tips introducing your new Scottish Fold to your existing pets can be as stress-free as possible.

6. Introducing your Scottish Fold to your dog

However, no matter what, always be present for the first introductions between a cat and dog. Ensure your dog is not feeling threatened and quash any aggressive behavior immediately. There are very few chances that your Scottish Fold will dislike or get intimidated by your pet dog. However, you cannot say the same for your pet dog. Breeds like the Labrador or the Golden Retriever are natural care givers. So, they will not harm your cat without reason, but other breeds can be less peaceful around an intruding animal. It is important for your dog to learn to obey commands. Special commands like 'Stay', 'Heel', 'Come' and 'Sit' must be familiar to your dog. If you have not trained your dog yet, make sure you start the process. You can also condition your dog to behave well with the cat by rewarding him every time he is well behaved with your cat. In the very early stages keep the dog and cat in separate rooms. The best way to ensure that they get used to each others' scent is to feed them on either side of the door of the room where the new cat is residing. If you feel like your dog is barking at or staring at the door or even scratching the door aggressively, don't force him to eat near the door.

The best idea is to set up a pen for your new cat, allowing the dog to sniff through the bars and grow accustomed to the new addition to the household. If the dog is more used to cats simply introducing your new cat in its carry case and allowing an introduction between the bars may suffice. Stroke both animals separately, without washing your hands in between, this will transfer their scent to one another and go some way to acclimatizing both pets to one another. Other good tips to acclimatize each other's scents is to switch the blankets or cushions of your pets or even placing the blanket of your cat next to the feeding bowl of your dog and vice versa. When outside be careful that the dog will not chase away your new cat, if they have already been properly introduced this should not happen but again, make sure any outside interactions are controlled at the beginning.

Irrespective of whether it is an introduction phase or not, never leave your cat and dog unleashed when there is no one at home. Unsupervised interactions can never be controlled entirely. Remember that your dog can kill your cat even with a playful bite. Especially if you are dealing with a kitten and a puppy, you must be very careful.

7. Introducing your Scottish Fold to your cat

Bringing two cats together can be slightly more problematic. It is stressful to your old pet to deal with the fact that there is another cat in the house. Quite obviously, it is stressful for you as well to make sure that your pet does not feel neglected or out of place. You need to take each step at a time to make the situation more relaxed for you, your older cat and the new Scottish Fold.

It is common for the cats to not get along immediately. If this is true for your resident cats and the new kitten, make sure you do not punish either of them. Just separate them when they get anxious. You must understand that this behavior is purely instinctive. With regular interactions, the cats will learn to live together peacefully.

Generally speaking, older cats will not feel threatened by kittens, as they are not sexually mature. Neutering may help prevent any difficulties with older cats and it may be better to bring in a cat of the opposite sex so there is no sense of competition. As with the dog, using a pen for initial introductions and petting both cats will help. Pens will allow the cats to smell each other and perhaps hiss or moan without the threat of aggression. Having a pen will also mean there is a safe place for the new cat or kitten when you leave the house so you don't have to worry about fighting or your new cat being harmed while you are away.

The interactions between your cats must be gradual. You can try the blanket switching from your current cat's bed to your new cats and vice-versa. When they are accustomed to each other's scent, they become comfortable with each other. You must allow them to spend more time with each other slowly. Only when you are assured that they are relaxed in each other's company, you can leave them unsupervised. Until then, you must never leave them unattended in the same space. This is especially true for night times.

A good technique to get your new cat and resident cat familiar with each other is to use food to bring them together. Hold off feeding until a little later than usual so you know they are hungry. Then bring your new cat and resident cat in to the room at the same time. Ensuring they have separate bowls allow them to feed close to each other but not so close that they invade each other's space. This technique will bring them out in the open together and the likelihood of them fighting straight after food is very slim so they will get used to each other's company.

Socializing two cats or a new cat with other pets may take just a day, it may take a few days or it could be a few months before they are comfortable with each other. Ultimately it all depends on the temperament of your pets, but these tips will hopefully make the transition easier for everyone. Luckily for you, Scottish Folds are perfect at adapting to ordinarily stressful situations, so hopefully your transition period will be as relaxed as possible.

8. Introducing your children or babies to your new cat

As has already been mentioned, Scottish Folds are more sensitive and tolerant towards children, compared to most other breeds. However, regardless of this, when you have brought home a new cat, it is quite possible that the children will get too excited and actually scare your new cat and cause them distress. Children may squeal or wail when they see the cat, which can be mistaken for aggression. A child looks, behaves and smells very different from an adult. This unfamiliarity could not only be distressing for your cat, it can also be dangerous for your child. There are some rules to introduce your child to the new cat.

Make sure your cat and child have regular interactions. At no point allow your child venture alone into your cat's room or area. You can teach your child to call the cat soothingly and even just watch the cat quietly till it gets accustomed to the presence.

As with other pets, scent is a very important thing when acclimatizing your new cat to your children. It would be a good idea to let your child handle some of your cat's items so that the scent is left behind for the cat to get used to. You can give your child one responsibility like handling the blanket of the cat or even just filling up the water bowl.

If you have a toddler at home, it is best not to assign duties quite yet. A better idea is to use the sock technique of introduction. All you need to do is rub a sock of the toddler on the cheek of the cat. Then, let the toddler wear the sock. Because of this rubbing of the scent, the cat will trust the toddler as a friend that she can trust.

Children must also be told that the cat is not a toy. You must constantly remind the child that pulling an ear or tail of the cat can be really painful for your cat.

9. Bringing home adult cats

Adult cats are very different from kittens. They will take longer to get used to the household and the people living there. This being said, the adaptability of Scottish Folds is a valuable thing, but just incase they have come from a less caring or volatile background they may need some help acclimatizing to their new surroundings. Your new Scottish Fold's behavior will depend entirely on the kind of interactions that he/she has had with people in the past. You can do a little background check and make necessary adjustments in your lifestyle to accommodate an adult cat. Whether you have rescued or adopted an older cat, there are simple tips and tricks that will help you make them feel comfortable.

- You must make sure you ask your breeder or the owner of the pet rescue center all the details of your cat's history. There may be specific toys that the cat is fond of. There may also be special scents or fragrances that the cat might require to feel comfortable. It is also important to know if your cat pet-to-be has had an abusive history. If yes, you must understand completely about the things that might make the cat anxious or uncomfortable.

- You can keep the adult cat in a cat carrier for a few days. In case there is a specific room for the new cat, make sure you leave the carrier there. This can become your cat's permanent hideout and also zone of comfort.

- The litter box, food and water must be introduced to the new adult cat. Place them all in their room or confinement room of the cat.

- When your cat is ready, you can take her to new parts of your home. It is absolutely mandatory that you familiarize the cat with all areas of your home. For indoor cats, being able to look for resting spots and hiding spots becomes possible only when she is comfortable with all the space available.

- With an adult cat, conditioning becomes necessary. You must make time to play with the cat, talk to him and just be around him. Some breeds require more attention than other cats, hopefully there will not be too many problems with the Scottish Fold but you still must try as hard as you can to keep him happy. Only when your cat is sure of you as the right companion he will open up and be friendly.

- Make sure you keep an eye on your new cat. If he does not eat properly or use the litter box, you might have to seek some help from an expert. Another common problem with adult cats is the development of skin problems. These are all signs of discomfort and unhappiness in the cat.

Adult cats have a wealth of experiences and interactions with other humans and animals behind them. So when introducing them to your home, remember patience is the most important virtue. But if they are shown love and care you will find they will settle well and you will get to know a cat with a fully-fledged personality.

Chapter 9: Feeding your Scottish Fold

Unfortunately there is a lack of concrete knowledge behind cat nutrition so you may hear some conflicting statements. Vets are not given full tuition on pet nutrition and a lot of the information they receive comes from pet-food companies. However, one thing can be agreed upon and that is your cat needs plenty of water, protein and nutrients. Scottish Folds do not have any special dietary requirements peculiar to the breed; they need just as many nutrients as any other cat.

The best way to give your cat a nutritional and well balanced diet is to cook the food yourself. This can seem laborious but it is definitely the most effective diet. However, a good mix of both dry and wet food and fresh fish and meat will do the trick if you do not have the time. Good recipes for homemade cat food can be found online but always ask yourself if your cat is getting all the nutrients they need.

1. What your Scottish Fold cat needs

Cats need a good balanced diet to stay healthy, much as humans do too! The following nutrients and vitamins will keep your Scottish Fold well nourished and balanced.

Water: Plenty of water readily available at all times is essential for all cats.

Protein: Cats need even more protein than dogs and you should make sure the food you give them has 20% protein at the very least.

Calcium: Just like with human babies, calcium is a vital part of a growing cat's healthy diet to help make their bones strong.

Fat: As with any foods, fat content gives the food better taste. But they are also vital for a cat's development. Fats are needed for energy, essential fatty acids and fat-soluble vitamin intake.

Vitamin A: Found in liver, eggs and milk this vitamin although essential should not be over-fed and should not comprise more then 10% of their diet.

Vitamin B: These are water-soluble vitamins and are important in a well-rounded diet. A lack of B-vitamins can result in a loss of appetite or anemia.

Vitamin E: Used to break down water-soluble fats, vitamin E can be difficult to judge. If your cat enjoys a lot of oily fish they will need an increased amount of vitamin intake.

2. The problems with dry food

Dry food is a very convenient product for pet owners as it can sit out for much longer than wet food and is much better value for money. However, with this convenience comes drawbacks, as you may not necessarily be giving your kitty all the nutrients and minerals they need if you let them eat just dry food.

Dry food does provide cats with nutrients but they are lower in protein and provide nowhere near enough water for a healthy cat. Cats need around 70% water levels in their system and cats on a dry food diet only have around 12%. This dehydration can lead to nasty urinary tract infections and other complications. The good thing about dry food is it encourages cats to not eat more carbohydrates than they need to, which do not mix well with cats.

It has been observed that dry foods are also cooked very harshly to provide the necessary texture and appearance. As a result, the nutritional value of these foods is greatly reduced. The amount of water consumed by a cat is the same whether you give it dry food or wet food. As a result, the total water consumed when the cat eats dry foods is reduced to almost half because there is no water present in the food itself.

Since the water consumed is substantially lower, the health hazards increase tremendously. Providing your cat with canned food is almost like flushing the digestive system. There are no risks of kidney and bladder related disorders if your cat consumes the recommended amount of water each day

In addition to this, cats are strict carnivores and get their protein most effectively from meat so it is essential you give your cat wet food. Many cat owners cite their cat is reluctant to eat wet food and is 'addicted' to dry, if this is the case there are some tips you can attempt to try and wean them off a purely dry food diet.

3. How to wean your cat off dry food

Transitioning from dry to wet food can take a long time so patience is key, but just remember you are doing what's best for your beloved Scottish Fold.

Firstly you need to set meal times and stop free-feeding dry food throughout the day. This may be difficult but a cat can go a few hours without eating and the hungrier they get the more likely they are to eat the wet food when you put it down. Establish meal times at about 2-3 times a day (there is no need for any less than this) and give them a combination of dry food and wet food. Using the hunger in your favor give them more wet food than dry and gradually over time give them more and more wet food until they have no dry food at all. This process can take a good few months and you may notice your cat loses weight a little but as long as they remain within their healthy weight this should be okay.

When you go to just wet food at some meal times your cat may turn their nose up at it, but persevere and resist the urge to put down dry food. In order to get them really hungry before mealtime play with them and force them to exert themselves even more than usual. It is also a good idea to get the dry food out of the way also. Either by moving it well away from their food bowls, putting it in a tightly sealed container, putting it in the fridge or all three! If they can smell the dry food they will hold out for it. Another tip to encourage them is to place some treat food on top of the wet food, such as canned fish or chicken.

4. Which food is best?

When choosing store-bought wet food, it is important you recognize the quality. Cheap pet foods are not necessarily nutritious and often you may find it is difficult to determine where the food has actually come from. There are several manufacturers who produce their foods in their own facilities and these companies are more trustworthy. The quality control is better as the sources of the ingredients and all the associated processes can be monitored effectively. All the foods that are manufactured on site are held until they meet all the safety guidelines recommended for the product. As a result, issues like Salmonella contamination can be prevented effectively.

In the US there is a good guideline that can be followed. According to the Association American Feed Control Officials, feeding trials are the most important tools to understand the quality of the pet foods. The pet foods that have undergone feeding trials are given to the pets under recommended guidelines. The guidelines are followed strictly to make sure that the animals get the right nutrition from them. When you buy any form of cat food, look for this sentence: "AAFCO procedures substantiate that this food provides complete and balanced nutrition".

When you purchase a certain cat food, check if the food has been 'manufactured by' or just has been 'distributed by' the brand that you are choosing. If the brand that you are purchasing is also the manufacturing unit, it is easier to register complaints with respect to the quality of the food provided. You can report all the concerns that you have on the quality of the food to the manufacturer directly.

There are several brands and types of cat foods available as per the activity level, age and breed of your cat. There are several "life stage foods" that have been formulated to suit the age of your cat. The nutritional requirements vary from kittens to adult and senior cats. However, there is another variety called the "ALL life stage" food. This is definitely not recommended as it may lead to malnutrition or even excessive nutrition, which could lead to several health issues in your cat.

If you find it hard to make a decision with the right food choice for your feline friend, you can simply take the help of store owners or salesmen who will know what is perfect for your cat. If you are still not convinced, the best person to talk to is your vet.

5. Tips for feeding your Scottish Fold

Ultimately, we all love our cats. We definitely want the best for them. However, sometimes, we make silly mistakes that may jeopardize the wellbeing of our cats. The most common mistakes made are associated with feeding. Here are three ways you can ensure that your cat gets complete and wholesome nutrition:

If unsure visit your vet: In case there are any negative reactions of certain foods on your cat's body, your vet will be able to point them out. They can also recommend necessary nutrients to assist your cat's current health conditions. If your cat has been put under a therapeutic diet, your vet will be able to enhance the diet as required. So, you must never skip visits to the vet if you want to ensure optimum nutrition for your cat.

Check the calories in the pet food: Whenever we buy processed foods for ourselves, we ensure that we check the nutrition chart on the packaging. We normally check for the calories and the fats that the particular food contains. The next time you buy some cat food off the rack for your cat ensure you do the same. Your cat must be put on a calorie conscious diet to make sure that she only receives the amount of calories he requires and nothing more. This precaution is necessary to make sure that your cat does not end up with unnecessary weight issues. Most pet foods that you can buy off the rack will have necessary details about the number of calories contained per serving.

These pet foods will also provide feeding guidelines that will tell you how you must provide your cat with a balanced diet. These guidelines are not always correct. If you are unsure of the serving size for your cat, the best person to talk to would be your vet. They will teach you how you can mix your cat's favorite treats with dry and mixed foods to keep his food interesting while maintaining a healthy weight.

Monitor how many treats you give your cat: Many pet owners make the mistake of giving their cats too many treats out of affection. The truth is that several confectionaries that you choose as suitable cat treats consist of large amounts of toxins that can be fatal for your cat.

Your cat may favor these treats, as they are very tasty, however, they are not of any nutritional value. Cats must be kept away from these treats, most importantly people food. You must allow a maximum of 10% of the cat's calorie intake to be from treats.

Giving them too many treats can lead to lack of nutrition and eventual dehydration.

Taking these three basic precautions will help you give your cat the best nutrition possible. It might be hard to get over bad feeding habits but you must put in a conscious effort, for the sake of your cat's health.

6. What not to feed your Scottish Fold cat

It does not need to be said that the kind of food that your cat eats and you eat are extremely different. The entire digestive ability is quite different and hence, the food should also be significantly different. Many pet owners make the mistake of giving their cats the same food that is cooked in their home, such as leftovers. However, just as you as a human would not consider snacking on their food; a cat should not generally be eating human food.

Usually pet owners think that their little beauties are sure of what is best for them. Cats are known to be picky eaters but there is little evidence that suggests that a cat knows what is right for it and what is wrong. Perhaps in the wild, cats follow their instincts and get the right nutrition. However, with domesticated cats, the varieties of foods that are available for them will make them reach out for all the wrong goodies.

Not only are human foods nutritionally poor, they can also be quite dangerous for your cat. However, this can be difficult to judge as cats will enjoy just about anything that you feed them. Operating under the assumption that your cat is happy, you may continue to give him foods that can have serious health related issues. Here are 15 foods that are a complete no-no for your beloved Scottish Fold cat:

Tuna: Although this does sound strange, there is a good chance that your cat will get addicted to tuna. Of course a share of tuna now and then should not harm your cat too much. However, a steady tuna diet can cause malnutrition. Although cats savor tuna and really enjoy it, the nutrients available are not too many. Another common issue with tuna is mercury poisoning. Never keep open tuna cans within the reach of your cat. You can serve it occasionally but make sure that she knows that it is not available all the time.

Chives, Garlic, Onion: These are common ingredients in all our foods but they have disastrous health impacts on cats. Any form of these vegetables, cooked, powdered or even raw can cause anemia in cats by completely breaking down their red blood cells. Even though human baby food consists of powdered onion, do not consider it safe for your cat. Onion poisoning and even gastrointestinal problems might arise if your cat eats chives, garlic or onion.

Dairy Products: Contrary to common belief, dairy products, including milk are not advised for cats. They are able to tolerate and digest milk only when they are kittens. In adult cats, the digestive system is unable to process dairy products and, therefore, health issues like diarrhea and other digestive issues become quite common.

Alcohol: Your cat must never ever consume any form of alcohol. Make sure that all the liquor in your home is out of your cat's reach. The effects on the cats' liver and brain are similar to the effects on the human brain. In cats, however, the amount of alcohol required to do this damage is a lot less. A 5lb cat can go into coma with just two teaspoons of liquor. Even one teaspoon more could potentially be fatal. In pedigrees the effect of alcohol is even worse.

Raisins and Grapes: Many cat owners consider grapes and raisins as suitable treats for their cats. This is never a good idea. Giving your cat too many raisins or grapes can eventually lead to kidney failure. Even a small share of grapes can really make your cat fall sick. Vomiting is one early sign of illness caused by grapes. Some cats may have no reactions but we are not sure of the long-term effects of feeding grapes to your cat.

Caffeine: An overdose of caffeine could actually kill your cat. With caffeine intake, there is no antidote either. The most common symptoms of caffeine poisoning in cats include:
- Restlessness
- Fast Paced Breath
- Palpitations in the heart
- Muscle tremors

Caffeine is not only found in coffee. There are several other sources including beans, chocolates, colas and even energy drinks like red bull. Some medicines and painkillers also contain substantial amounts of caffeine.

Chocolate: It is impossible to say no to your adorable cat staring at you while you gorge on chocolate. However, this treat can end up being extremely harmful for your cat. Chocolate consists of a toxic material known as theobromine; this is extremely dangerous for cats. It is found in all forms of chocolate including white chocolate. The common problems associated with chocolate are:
- Muscle tremors
- Seizures
- Abnormality in heart rhythm
- Death

Candy: Any sweetened food including candy, gum, toothpaste and baked goods contain an element called xylitol. This element can pace up the circulation of insulin in the cat's body. As a result, the level of sugar in the cat's body drops suddenly causing seizures and liver failure in your cat.

Bones and Fat Trimmings: Scraps from the table are fed so often to cats but fat and bone can cause serious health disorders in cats. Fat, whether cooked or uncooked, can result in vomiting, diarrhea and intestinal problems in your cat. If a cat chokes on a bone, it can be fatal. Other problems related to the bones are lacerations and obstructions due to the splinters.

Raw Eggs: Many people believe that raw eggs are a healthy dietary option for their cat. However, this is not true. There are two primary health issues that result from consumption of raw eggs. Firstly, food poisoning may occur due to the presence of bacteria like E coli. Secondly, a certain protein in the egg white, known as avidin can reduce the absorption of vitamin B in cats leading to skin related issues.

Raw Meat: Although many may argue that cats only eat raw meats in the wild, the truth is that uncooked meat and fish can be harmful to cats. They contain bacteria and microorganisms that might cause food poisoning. Additionally, certain enzymes present in raw fish can destroy essential vitamins like thiamine in the cat's body. This can cause neurological problems and can also result in coma in extreme cases.

Dog Food: A bite once in a while will not harm your cat too much. However, the formula used in dog food is definitely not suitable for cats. Cat food is packed with necessary proteins and vitamins that can help the cat fulfill its nutritional requirements. On the other hand, dog foods can also contain plant proteins that are not suitable for your cat. If your cat regularly consumes dog food, it might become malnourished.

Liver: Giving your cat liver once in a while is not an issue. However, too much consumption of liver can lead to vitamin A toxicity in cats. This is a serious condition as it affects the bones. There might be deformities and also bone growths and spurts on the spine. Osteoporosis can also be observed in cats with vitamin A toxicity. In extreme cases it can be fatal.

Yeast Dough: Uncooked dough is never recommended for a cat. If the cat consumes it, there are chances that the dough will actually raise inside the cat's stomach. During this expansion, the dough may stretch the abdomen on the cat and also cause alcohol poisoning as the yeast ferments.

Many times, being cautious isn't good enough. Your cat might just make its way into your pantry and have a generous helping of restricted foods. There is no need to be alarmed. In most cases, your vet will be able to provide an antidote to take care of the situation for you.

It is also worth noting that if you notice something is strange with your cat, either they go off their food or their litter tray habits change they could have eaten something that does not agree with them. Before taking them to the veterinary clinic, have a check in your food cupboard and elsewhere to ensure they have not eaten something they shouldn't have. If you find some clues this may help your veterinarian provide the best course of treatment.

Chapter 10: Grooming Your Cat

Anyone that observes their cat at all will notice they take care of their own grooming very well. About 2 to 3 times a day they will clean their coat themselves. However sometimes they will need a little assistance from their owner.

1. Grooming tasks

Brushing your cat: Scottish Folds can have short, medium or long hair. Their coat is quite dense and the longhaired cats will need much more grooming than the shorter, to avoid matting. Brushing your cat helps prevent molting. Usually longhaired cats will need much more brushing as they have a lot more hair, which needs shedding. Use a metal comb and work through the hair from head to tail. Using a bristle or rubber brush take up any extra hair. For longhaired Scottish Folds the process will be a little longer and make sure to work through their belly and legs to detangle any knots. It is important you keep grooming sessions short if your cat is particularly stressed or anxious, especially at the beginning. You want your cat to associate brushing with a positive emotion and not something to be endured.

There are several benefits of brushing your Scottish Fold cat's coat; a good, thorough brushing once a week will help:

- Improve blood circulation

- Add more sheen to the fur

- Remove loose hairs, if any

- Remove dried skin to keep the fur healthy

- Remove parasites, if any.

Although brushing may seem like a very ordinary task, if done right, the benefits will be multiplied:

- Make sure all the strokes are even and in the direction of the fur. This will help eliminate the loose hairs and actually massage the cat's body.

- Using a cat hairbrush, brush off all the loose hairs for your cat's body.

- You can even use your grooming gloves to get rid of any debris that is visible on your cat's coat.

- Your cat's skin consists of several natural oils. Massaging the body thoroughly after brushing will help distribute this oil evenly across the cat's body to produce healthier and shiner fur.

- Your cat's skin is very thin. So make sure the bristles of the brush are not too sharp. You must also ensure that you do not apply too much pressure while brushing the fur. It can cause cuts and bruises more easily in shorthaired cats.

Cleaning the folded ears: Many Scottish Fold owners are tempted to clean inside their ears. In truth, this is not completely necessary. Just like human ears, cat ears are in themselves, self-cleaning. It is good to keep and eye on them though and check for any build up of dirt. If you do notice something take some warm water and a cotton ball and very carefully clean them. If your cat struggles too much, do not force them. If you start to worry, take your cat to the vet and they may be able to recommend the next step. Never use a Q-tip/Ear bud unless specifically advised to by your vet, these can be pushed in too far and cause pain and potential infections for your Scottish Fold.

You can purchase ear cleansers, which you can add one drop to your kitty and then wait for the dirt or wax to dislodge on its own. Any type of ear cleaning should be conducted with praise and treats, this will relax your Scottish Fold and hopefully make the process much easier.

Earwax or dirt should be dry and either slightly yellow or brown. When inspecting your cat's ears they should not have any liquid or bright yellow pus. If you notice anything unusual do not touch the ears yourself. Take them to the vet and they will be treated for either bacterial or fungal infection of maybe a mite infestation.

Nail Clipping: If your cat's claws are getting too long and start splitting you may wish to clip their nails. This is much more humane than having your cat declawed (which will be discussed in more detail later) and with a little patience it does not have to be the ordeal you might expect. Firstly you may have to spend some time getting your cat used to you petting its feet. Do this when they are relaxed and at the same time as stroking their favorite spots, maybe on their cheek or belly. Once your cat allows you to touch the top of their paw without moving it away you should start trying to gently squeeze the paws. This can be a long process but it is much better than going in with the clippers straight away, with fewer scratches for you! When your cat is relaxed with you touching their feet you can start clipping. Do this when they are relaxed, perhaps just before a nap. Pet nail clippers are available at most pet stores and will be the only way to clip your cat's claws effectively. Begin by just taking a little off the top and then getting closer to the quick; do not touch the quick or you may hurt them. If you do cut the quick by accident quickly apply styptic powder to prevent infection. Once you are finished clipping the nails give your cat a treat so they will be less resistant in the future.

2. Declawing

Many pet owners may consider declawing as a suitable grooming technique. This is a surgical procedure that removes the claws of the cat entirely. Also known as onychectomy, the procedure involves the removal of the end bones of the cat's toes partly or entirely. This is a practice that is very common in North America. However, because of the effects it has on the cat and its well-being, it is also considered animal cruelty in many parts of the world.

This practice is followed in order to prevent the cat from damaging furniture and property. Other pet owners also justify declawing a cat as a method of protecting other people from being scratched or hurt by their cat. In many apartments, people are not allowed to keep cats unless they are completely declawed. It is quite certain that these people do not understand the seriousness of this procedure. It is not a way of keeping the nails trimmed or blunt. It is a medical surgery that has untoward repercussions on the cat. The toenails of your cat are attached very closely to its bones so removing the claw is as good as amputating the toes of your cat. The period of recovery is extremely painful and there is also no guarantee that your beloved pet will recover entirely from this traumatic experience. For this reason, several European countries have strong laws against declawing cats.

If you have considered declawing or it has been suggested to you, it is essential that you understand the procedure and the aftermath of the surgery on your cat. To help you understand better, here are some drastic problems that your cat will face during the period of recovery:

Physical Discomfort: Remember that your cat will not lose its instinctive behavior even if it is in pain. She will still want to jump, scratch and even play despite the pain and she will also have to use the litter box. Recovery time can vary but generally speaking for up to 3 days, you will notice lameness in your cat. She will drag herself to go through with her routine.

Almost 80% of cats that have undergone declawing have shown signs of complications after surgery. While the complications developed post surgery in some, others reported issues after release. These complications were caused due to wrong sheering techniques or even the blade used for surgery.

The most common medical conditions include abscesses, necrosis of tissues, growth of deformed claws, motor paralysis, nerve damage, hemorrhage, and bladder inflammation due to stress, infections, swelling and even reluctance to walk.

Behavior Changes: When declawing, owners often remark that the personality of their cat changes. There are valid reasons to support this change in behavior and personality of the cat. The biting frequency and strength increases in most cats and the only possible explanation for this is that when a cat loses one form of defense, it activates another.

House soiling is also twice as common in declawed cats as they are reluctant to use their litter tray due to their heightened sensitivity. They become reluctant to walk and put pressure on their paws and in addition to that, severe cases like nerve dysfunction and even lameness renders the cat quite helpless.

Aggression is also very common in cats post declawing. The pain makes them more defensive against people and the fact that you as the owner inflicted that pain upon her, makes you less trustworthy in the eyes of your cat.

Almost 45% of cats that have been declawed are referred to vet teaching hospitals and cat schools to sort out behavioral issues. The change in behavior is more drastic if the cat has undergone tendonectomy in the process of being declawed. The repercussions of these behavior changes include relinquishing cats to shelters.

Reasons not to Declaw: By now, you will have understood how painful the experience of declawing is for your cat.

When you declaw a cat, you are essentially maiming it. This can lead to several emotional, behavioral and physical complications. The claws of the cat are an essential part of its anatomy and your cat requires its claws to stay mobile, to balance itself and to also defend itself from predators.

The process of declawing is irreversible and by amputating the bone ends of the cat, you are subjecting it to potential disability. Secondary complications that come with this surgical procedure cannot be undone.

Very rarely, contracture of tendons occurs due to declawing. This makes it difficult for the cat to walk properly; they tend to rest all their weight on their hind legs, as their front paws are actually missing. This type of imbalance may result in muscle atrophy.

These conditions can lead to your cat becoming increasingly stressed and unhappy. Like we all know, cats tend to jump off high counters, trees and even leap up to incredible heights. With a primary organ responsible for their ability to balance missing, cats tend to become very distressed.

Although declawing seems like a viable option for indoor cats, you cannot guarantee your cat will never venture outside. In the event of this, by declawing your cat, you are making her entirely defenseless in an environment that can be hostile. Even though claws sometimes grow back after 15 years, it might be crooked and deformed. So with no chance of replacement, you are practically stripping your cat of its primary defense mechanism.

Emotional distress is highly prevalent in cats that have been declawed also. The most obvious signs of being upset are urinating on a rug that you love the most or even knocking down an antique object. Cats become very hostile to people in general and will bite more often when you have taken away one of their main defense mechanisms.

One common habit of a cat is to scratch the sand in their litter box. When they are declawed, they will find this activity extremely painful. As a result, your cat will become averse to the litter box and they may find alternate places to do their business. If your cat develops this habit, you will find it extremely hard to break.

So, if you are still concerned about your cat's sharp claws causing damage to people and property, you can look for alternatives.

Declawing alternatives: We have already discussed trimming your cat's nails, but there are other options available. Another simple option is to provide your cat with a scratching post. You can attract your cat to the scratching post by using scent sprays that use catnip. A sisal scratch post is most recommended for cats as the roughness of the surface is just right for the cat to fulfill its urge to scratch something.

One of the simplest and most effective solutions is Soft Paws. This is a nail cap made of vinyl that you can simply glue to the front claws of your cat. It is best recommended for those who have cats that spend most of their time indoors. You can even protect your children from the cat with the help of Soft Claws. What is best is that Soft Paws comes in a variety of colors as well if you want to experiment and give your kitty a nice manicure. Once these caps wear off, they can be simply replaced with a new set.
Train your cat. That is the best way to protect your space and others from the claws of the cat. Teach your cat to only use the scratch post. You can also train it to be at its best behavior when it is around strangers.

For indoor cats, all the above alternatives work fine. If you have an outdoor cat, you might want to avoid clipping the nails or even using nail caps so that your cat can be on guard in the event of a fight.

3. Bathing your cat

If your cat has been out and has rolled in to something sticky or smelly you may wish to give them a bath. For long haired breeds you may wish to bathe them more regularly as their hair can be a potential breeding ground for germs. This should not be too necessary when your cat is younger, but as they age you may find they struggle to clean themselves effectively. Cats are not fans of water and will find the event fairly stressful so be sure to treat them once it is over.

Cats usually give themselves a good clean up and keep their coat spotless by licking off all the dirt. So many pet owners argue that their cat does not require a bath regularly. However, this is not always the case, there are several reasons in fact, why your cat may require a bath:

- It can be necessary to keep her coat clean and free from ticks and fleas.
- The amount of oil on the skin is reduced.
- They tend to climb up chimneys and really soil themselves.
- A vet may recommend a bath to help your cat recover from specific health conditions.

When you are giving your cat a bath, remember that you cannot leave her unsupervised for even one second until she is ready to be wrapped in a towel and dried up. So, you must keep all the necessary supplies handy to avoid having to walk in and out of the cat's bathing area. The best way to ensure an uninterrupted bath is to make a checklist of all the necessary supplies. Here is a quick look at the things you will need to give your cat a bath:

- Cat Shampoo
- A pitcher or spray nozzle to rinse the cat
- Rubber Gloves to prevent injuries to the cat because of your nails

- Cotton balls to clear up the ears
- A large towel to dry her off
- A small towel to just clean his face

Many people choose to give their cats a bath in the tub. This is not the best option as bending over the tub can really strain your back and give you a hard time. It also provides a lot of space for your cat to escape and when bending over a bathtub you will not have as much control over the situation. Cue a very messy bathroom!

So, the best and least messy way is to bathe them in a sink or raised baby bath. Cleaning up afterwards will also be easier when you choose this option. You can follow step by step instructions to give your cat a bath that is painless and relaxed.

- Fill the tub or the sink with warm water. You must make sure that the water is not too hot or too cold. The water must be 2 or 3 inches deep if you have an adult cat. For a kitten just an inch depth will do.
- Avoid a faucet or a jar to pour water on the cat. You can gently wet the cat and then make a good lather with the shampoo.
- You must treat your cat's coat in the same way as you would treat your own hair. You must rinse the shampoo off gently and make sure that it is entirely gone. Leaving traces of the shampoo on the coat might lead to unwanted infections.
- During the entire bathing process, prevent splashing water on your cat's face. Cats simply hate this. Instead, you can just use a damp wash cloth to wipe the face and clean the ends of the cat's mouth.
- To clean the ears of a cat, just use a soft cotton ball. Never put objects like a Q tip or other pointed objects in to your cat's year. Even a slight squirm or nudge can cause serious injuries to your cat.

- When you are done bathing her, cover with a large towel. Dry off as much water as possible. With a little rubbing with the towel, your cat will be fully dry.

When you give your cat a bath, make sure you use a good cat shampoo. In case you run out of it and don't have time to go to the pet store, you can just use a baby shampoo. Never use any cleaning product on your cat as it will irritate the skin and eyes.

Chapter 11: Transporting Your Cat

1. Before your journey

Taking a cat anywhere can always seem like a daunting prospect. Luckily, as we have already mentioned, Scottish Folds are not easily flappable and adapt well to strange experiences. However, this is by no means a rule and most cats find being moved around very stressful.

More often than not you will want to transport your cat for veterinary visits. This means your cat may associate their cat box with negative connotations. It is a good idea to always keep the carry case close by to their other items so it is associated with home and comfort for them. Line the tray with a towel or blanket that has their scent on it and when you reach your destination pull the towel out to help coax them out again.

Most cats dislike cars. So most of the resistance to the visit to the vet is not the clinic itself, it has more to do with the journey to the vet. Usually, cats are taken out in the car only during their visit to the vet. As a result, they automatically associate cars with the negative experiences that they might have had at the vet, including injections and bad tasting medicines. So cats can never stay calm and relaxed inside a car.

However, you can help your cat to make positive associations by including drives in the car in your daily routine. You can take the car for short distances too. Take the car to the park, for instance. Then your cat will stop making negative associations. You can even stop by at the vet's clinic for 5 minutes to get your cat used to the staff there.

The basic idea is to get your cat used to the car. He must learn to be calm and relaxed during these visits. Keeping some toys in the car and allowing him to play during these drives will also help a great deal.

Once again, journeys can be stressful for a cat so anything you can do to turn it in to a positive experience is a bonus; give treats when they get in to the carry case and then again when you return home.

2. Travelling by train

When you are travelling by train, you must obviously place your cat in a carrier. Since there will be strangers on a train, you do not want to have any instances of your cat breaking free and scaring them.

So, make sure that the carrier that you have is extremely sturdy. The base of the carrier must be extremely strong to ensure that your cat is secured. The carrier must be light so that you do not have any difficulty carrying it around. It must also be of a convenient size depending upon the space available on the train. Make sure that you get a carrier that is large enough for your cat to rest in. Never cram your kitty into a small carrier because there isn't enough storage space.

You must keep a familiar blanket in the carrier to reduce anxiety. However, littering and soiling can be quite a concern. So, line your cat's cage with a good amount of absorbent paper so that you may both have a pleasant journey.

3. Travelling by air

Travelling with your pet by air requires a good deal of planning in advance. The airlines that you choose will also vary with regards to their efficiency in handling and transferring your cat. Check with your airline first and ensure they will even agree to transport your breed of cat. Some breeds that are prone to respiratory problems are not suitable for flying, in which case many airlines refuse to carry them. Essentially it is recommended that you avoid air travel if you can help it. However, if you do find an airline that has the facility to transport your cat, you must take several precautions.

Cats will have very little trouble travelling by air. If you have a pregnant cat or a kitten under three months of age travelling with you, it might become a matter of concern. It is recommended that you avoid air travel for these two categories of cats.

Check for a license to transport animals in the airlines that you choose. Chances are that you and your cat will travel by separate flights. If this is true, make sure that you get a direct flight for your cat so that it does not have to deal with issues like transits and transfers.

4. Leaving your cat at home

Whether you are going on a vacation or even going out on a business trip, the biggest issue that you will face is making the right arrangements for your cat while you are away. Scottish Folds need company and being left alone will be hugely stressful for them. You must ensure that your cat is in safe hands and is somewhere where he will be treated well and given a lot of love and affection. There are several options that are available, but the most common and reliable ones are:

Friends: If you are a cat lover, you must be in the company of several others who love and adore cats. There will definitely be someone in your group who can pitch in to take care of your cat while you are away. This is also advisable as your Scottish Fold may already be familiar with their scent and would have encountered them before. When you are handing this responsibility over to a friend, make sure that he or she has had pets in the past, preferably a cat. You must look for someone who will be able to make your cat comfortable and less anxious.

Family: If you have relatives who visit you regularly, leaving your cat in their care is a great idea. Just as with friend, this is because your cat will be familiar with their smell and sight and will be able to adjust better in their company. If someone from your family is willing to stay over at your place and take care of your cat while you are away, it is the best possible deal.

Ask your Neighbor: If you have friendly neighbors who love cats, request they take care of yours. Neighbors, again, will be familiar with your cat and will therefore be able to comfort your cat while you are away. Not just that, the locality and the surroundings will not be too different for your cat to make adjustments to.

Find a pet sitter: There are plenty of companies who will be willing to provide you with pet sitting services while you are away. Before you narrow down on one particular company, make sure that you are aware of the choices that you have before you. You can ask for recommendations from people who have availed these services in the past to choose the right company for your cat.

Meet the people at the company to understand their temperament and their ability to deal with cats. If you are sure that they are gentle, kind and, most importantly, responsible, you can do a trial run for one evening. If you see that they are good with your cat and that your cat is comfortable in their presence, you can give them the responsibility of taking care of your loved one while you are away.

Find a boarding home/cattery: There are several places where your cat will be boarded for the period that you are away. These professionals have all the necessary assistance. From people who feed and clean the cages to certified veterinarians, you will sometimes find that all the services are provided in these shelters. Of course, you can ask for recommendations before you actually decide to place your cat in a particular shelter. Make a visit to these places to check their standards of hygiene. The conditions of the cages, the staff available and the facilities available play an important role in the decision that you make.

If you have to travel, leaving your Scottish Fold home alone, make sure that you take all the necessary measures to schedule your trip according to your cat. Plan well in advance and keep a list of options that are available to take care of her. Never rush these things as you will end up making compromises on the necessary arrangements.

You can never say when an emergency will occur. In case you have to leave suddenly, you must be able to find the best assistance for your cat's care. So, it is a good idea to make a list of people who will always be willing to take care of your cat while you are away. It is a good idea to make a chart of possible contacts and keep them near your phone so you can just reach out, pick up the phone and make sure your cat has a safe home to stay in.

If you are someone who works late hours, you might want to look for someone else to keep your cat company while you are away. If it is only occasionally that you get held up at work, you can just call someone from your caretakers' list to ensure that the cat is not alone. You must also make sure that there is someone to feed your cat on time when you are away.

If you frequently stay away from home, you can get yourself a pet monitor. These interesting devices will help you call out to your cat and also watch her all day long. Some modern devices also allow you to time a dispenser that will pop out treats as and when required. That way, your cat will never feel like she is at home all by herself.

You could hire a full-time caretaker for your cat if you think it would be necessary. Make sure that you conduct a thorough interview before you actually appoint someone to take care of your cat. Inform this person about all the schedules of your cat. If your cat is under special medication or even a special diet, the caretaker must be informed well in advance.

The last option is to keep multiple pets at home. You can bring home another cat and allow your current pet and the new pet to get acquainted with each other. If you are just about to bring a pet into your home, a very good plan would be to just bring home two of them at once. They will grow up together and be able to keep each other company.

No matter what you do, the bottom line is that cats do not like to be left all alone at home for too long. Even if it takes a great deal of effort from your end, make sure you keep your cat company whether you are gone for a couple of hours, or for days on end.

Chapter 12: When Your Scottish Fold Cat Is ill

1. How to tell if your cat is ill

Upon observing and getting to know your cat you should have learned its habits and routine. If you feel they are acting differently than normal this could possibly be a sign that they are ill.

There are a number of signs that may point towards health problems that should be checked by a vet straight away. Here we have listed a few of these signs.

A loss of appetite could point to some health problems. If your cat goes more than 24 hours without eating take them to the vet for a check up.

Changes in their litter box habits could possibly indicate feline urinary tract disease (FUTD). This can be painful and if left untreated could become fatal. Check for frequent urination, blood in the urine, loss of appetite and licking of the genitals. If you suspect FUTD take them to your vet immediately.

An altered body language such as dizziness, head tilting and a seemingly disoriented nature may be signs of a neurological disorder.

If it seems like your cat's personality has changed you may have cause for suspecting an illness. If they have suddenly stopped playing or exercising and tend to sleep a lot more than usual they may be undernourished. Take your cat to the vet and let them know what you are feeding them. They may be able to suggest which nutrients are missing from your cats diet.

If you notice excessive discharge from your cat's eyes and nose they may be suffering some kind of allergic reaction. If this discharge is combined with excessive drinking and urination they could be suffering from kidney failure.

Cats can be prone to lumps and unusual growths. Most of the time these tend to be benign but if you notice oozing or tenderness they will need checking by a vet.

Dilated pupils are common, however they should not be constantly dilated and if they remain so for a prolonged period there could be something wrong.

Shallow or heavy breathing is common if your cat has just been playing or running around. However, you should take them to your vet if they are breathing like this without having exercised. On top of all of these typical signs you will get to know your cat and if you feel something is not right take them to the vet.

Shedding: Shedding is a common problem with many cat breeds. It is a common process by which cast lose their dead hair. In an indoor cat shedding is not a seasonal affair and it will occur all year long. If left unattended, you will notice cat hair everywhere. From the furniture to your wardrobe, your cat's hair will make its way to all corners of your home.

Regular grooming is one of the best ways to minimize shedding of your cat's fur, which we have already discussed. However, while shedding is not a medical problem per say, there are some special cases when you must alert your vet about the shedding of your cat's hair. Shedding is a matter of grave concern when:

- Bald patches begin to appear on the skin
- Your cat obsessively scratches or licks a particular area
- The amount of hair loss is a lot more than usual.

In such cases, shedding might be due to:

- Ringworm infections
- Allergies
- Infection by bacteria
- Fleas
- Hormonal problems
- Prescribed medication
- Stress
- Imbalanced diet
- Poor grooming and hygiene
- Pregnancy

If there is a medical cause for the shedding, your vet will be able to provide you with the necessary remedy. Once this course of treatment is over, you can follow some simple steps to keep your cat's shedding under control.

- Keep an eye on your cat's skin when you are grooming her

- Groom regularly

- Make sure your cat gets a proper, balanced diet.

With these precautions, you will be able to take good care of your Scottish Fold's lovely, dense coat.

2. Taking your cat to the vet

First and foremost it is essential you have a good veterinarian to take your cat to. A good idea is to visit your local veterinary surgeries and get a feel for them before taking your cat.

It is never a good idea to constantly change your vet from one visit to the next, as you know, cats do not appreciate change. They are usually reluctant to cooperate with vets so, you must give your cat time to get accustomed to the touch and voice of one vet. Once she is comfortable with him or her, your cat will be more relaxed during her vet visits. Your vet will become an important part of your cat's life and you must make sure you look for the perfect one to take care of your pet.

There are often several large and small veterinary clinics in any given area so, it can be quite confusing when you set out to choose which surgery is right for you. The best way to look for a vet is to ask for recommendations from your friends and neighbors. If you know people in the neighborhood who have had pets for a long time, they will be able to recommend someone to you.

You must make a conscious effort to look for someone who is specialized in cat care. This section of veterinary care is growing rapidly and you should definitely find someone in your chosen vicinity.

It is also good to consider basic logistics when choosing a veterinarian. In order to be prepared for an emergency, here are some things that you might want to consider before you zero in on one vet:

- How far is your vet from your home?
- Is the commuting time too long?
- In case of an emergency, will you make it on time to the vet?
- Is the ambience of the clinic feasible for your cat?

It is always better to find a vet as close to your house as possible. It must not take more than 15 minutes to drive to them; even if it is not an emergency most cats are not particularly fond of long drives.

Once you have found someone who seems to fit into all the requirements, you can make a trial visit. The chemistry between your cat and the vet is extremely important if you want to make it a long lasting relationship. There are some signs that will indicate how comfortable you and your pet will be in a particular clinic and how well the clinic is run. Make the following observations if you are visiting for the first time.

- The waiting room must be well maintained
- The ambience must be comforting for the cat so that she feels secure when he is being examined
- If it is a common clinic for dogs and cats, how are they maintained when they are admitted for hospital care? Are they kept in separate cages?
- The people at the reception must be friendly. These people are going to be your point of contact in the coming sessions and you must be comfortable with them.

Once you are in the examination room, check how the vet interacts with pets and their owners. The tone must be soothing. They must be able to provide undivided attention to your cat and must value your opinions about your cat's health and must be respectful towards you.

Once you are assured of the behavior of the vet towards you and your cat, you need to get down to the technical and legal aspects

- Is the facility adept in handling emergencies?
- How many cages or rooms do they have for the pets that have been admitted there?
- Is every staff member educated?
- Is the facility licensed?
- What are the costs for tests and surgeries?
- Is the pricing competitive enough?
- What are the insurance policies that they accept?
- How many emergencies are handled after regular working hours?
- Who takes care of the pets when they are hospitalized?
- Are they open to alternative medicines and treatments?

Once you have received satisfactory answers to all the above questions, you can be assured that this facility is best suited for your cat. The next step is to convince your cat of the same!

We have already discussed transporting your cat but once you get to the vet you may still face some difficulties. Your cat will be able to sense the other animals in the area and so will already be feeling apprehensive before you even get to see your vet. When you arrive try and find a quiet space in the waiting room. One place dreaded by all animals is the waiting room at the clinic. There are several unpleasant sounds like the barking of dogs and even chatter of humans that increase the levels of anxiety in a cat. Cats are, by nature, solitary animals and do not like being introduced to so many strange sights and sounds at one go. The best thing to do would be to leave your cat in the carrier till she is called in for examination. This gives her a secure hide out and she will be more at ease. If there are no quiet spaces and the waiting room is crowded perhaps wait outside or in your car before your appointment.

Once you get on to the veterinarian's table try and coax your cat out of the carry case as gently as possible. Your vet will have plenty of experience handling nervous animals so if your cat does not come out straight away feel free to let the vet take over. As was mentioned before, try bringing out the towel or blanket you have used to line the case and putting them on top of this. That way they have a smell of home with them at all times. This is also essential if your cat has to spend a night at the clinic.

3. Some common health problems with cats

Hairballs

One of the most unpleasant sights with longhaired cats in particular is that of them spitting out hairballs. The way a cat gags and snorts as it spews the hairball can break your heart. Although you cannot prevent hairballs entirely, you can take several precautions to make sure that hairballs do not turn into your Scottish Fold's worst nightmare.

They can cause intestinal infections that can be a major health threat to your cat. Now, it is impossible to prevent your cat from grooming himself. However, there are some simple measures that you can take to make sure that the occurrence of hairballs is controlled effectively.

Causes of Hairballs: The only cause of hairballs is the grooming routine that your cat carries out every day. Grooming and preening is a cat's second nature and there is nothing you can do to control it or stop it. Usually, when a cat licks itself, the loose hair that may be present will be picked up by tiny hook like structures present on the cat's tongue. Usually, the hair is able to pass through the digestive system. Sometimes, however, some strands stay back in the stomach and accumulate as the cat continues to groom itself.

You may have noticed that the problem of hairballs increases as your cat grows older. This is because the grooming routine becomes more rigorous with age. In case your cat sheds fur too often, there are chances of hairballs being formed in the stomach.

Symptoms of Hairballs: The most common symptoms are retching and gagging. However, there are some prominent symptoms that you will notice when hairballs are forming inside the cat's stomach:

- Lethargy

- Constant vomiting

- Sudden loss of appetite

- Diarrhea

- Constipation

Of course, you cannot stop your cat from grooming itself. However, there are precautions you can take to ensure that the number of loose hairs is reduced:

- Make sure you groom your cat regularly. You must brush longhaired cats for at least 15 minutes each day. The loose hairs must be brushed off thoroughly to reduce the chances of strays.

- You can use cat food with hairball formula to reduce the retention of hair in your cat's stomach.

- You may give a recommended laxative to your cat to ease the process of digestion.

Fleas: Fleas are not just an issue with dogs. They are very often seen in cats. In case of darker coats, they are even more difficult to locate because of the color of the cat's fur. This is an external health issue that can be treated easily. The signs of a flea invasion include:

- Constant scratching of the skin
- Irritated and Inflamed skin
- Frequent licking
- Sudden Hair loss
- Visually prominent skin infections

If left untreated, fleas can make a home in your pet's coat for years and can cause anemia if left untreated. Sudden weight loss and even loss of appetite are indications that fleas are attacking your cat. There are several powders, topical medicines and also foams that are available to treat fleas.

If the problem persists, it is best to see your vet for oral medicines to get rid of the condition permanently. Sometimes, the treatment is not restricted to the fleas alone. You might have to even treat your cat for skin infections and even eating disorders resulting from the presence of fleas in the skin for a long time.

Tapeworms: An internal infection by tapeworms can be hazardous to your cat's health. These parasites usually invade the intestines of cats and can grow up to 2 feet in length if left untreated. Tapeworm infections have very subtle symptoms. This is why you must always keep a close watch on your cat to ensure that the problem of tapeworms does not go undetected. The symptoms include:

- Sudden weight loss
- Vomiting
- Presence of small, white worms in the feces and in the anal region

The last symptom is the only sure shot way of saying if your cat really is infected by tapeworms. This problem is usually linked with the presence of fleas on your cat's coat. Ingesting a flea can result in an infection by tapeworms. It is important to handle fleas as well when you are tackling the issue of tapeworms. The most common modes of treatment include tropical medication, oral medicines and injections.

Diarrhea: There are several reasons for cats to develop diarrhea. Some of the most common causes include:

- Liver disease
- Intake of spoiled food
- Allergies
- Ingestion of loose hairs
- Cancer

The symptoms of diarrhea include loose stools. They are usually watery in nature. Diarrhea can last for up to 6 months depending upon the causal factors.

The biggest problem with diarrhea is dehydration. Therefore it is mandatory to give your cat plenty of fresh, clean water to consume. You must also reduce the quantity of food given to your cat for about 24 hours. If diarrhea continues and is accompanied by loss of appetite, lethargy, bloody stools and fever, you must take your cat for evaluation by a veterinarian.

Feline Lower Urinary Tract Infection: Feline Lower Urinary Tract Infection affects almost 10% of cats. There are multiple causes for this disorder, which is actually a group of disorders that affect cats commonly. It is possible for both female and male cats to suffer and it is most often stress related. In other cases, cats that eat dry foods might suffer from this condition due to a lack of water intake. Feline Lower Urinary Tract Disorder is very common in cats that are unhealthy and overweight and it is also possible for a cat in a multi-cat home to develop this condition due to territorial issues. The symptoms for Feline Lower Urinary Tract Disorder are:

- Too much strain during urination
- Traces of blood in the urine
- Urination in places that are unusual
- Loud Purrs and cries while urinating
- Constant licking in the urinary area to reduce the pain
- Depression
- Sudden Dehydration
- Loss of appetite
- Constant vomiting

The treatment for Feline Lower Urinary Tract Infection depends on the cause and the type of infection. The inability to urinate is a matter of great concern in pets. You must call your vet immediately if you observe one or more of the above symptoms.

Chapter 13: Some Common Health Problems With Scottish Fold Cats

As Scottish Fold is a fairly new breed there is a lot we don't know for sure but the below are diseases that have occurred in the breed. Some of which are more prevalent than others but you should be on guard to spot all of them.

1. Osteochondrodysplasia (OCD)

It is this disease that caused the Scottish Fold to be withdrawn from shows in its home nation in 1979. All Scottish Folds born with the distinctive folded over ears have the disease to one extent or the other.

The fold in the Scottish fold is due to a defect in the cartilage that displays itself in areas without bone, where cartilage is needed to support the structure, i.e. the ear. This defect also affects the bones and, by extension, the joints. Cartilage is needed to support the bones at the joints, if there is a defect in the cartilage it means movement at the joints can be very painful. This can eventually develop in to arthritis.

Despite breeding folded ear cats with non-folded ear cats, the disease is present in both forms and recommendations have suggested that any breeding with folded ear cats should be ceased to stop the disease completely.

Symptoms of Osteochondrodysplasia (OCD)

As mentioned, all Scottish Folds with the folded ears will develop OCD at some point, usually early in life. Symptoms for this include:

- The development of deformity, with wide, short limbs;

- Struggling to move and suffer incredible pain.
- In some cases deafness in the left ear is also reported.

The disease can be easily tested for when kittens by examining their tail as mentioned previously. This is an extreme case however, some cats only suffer mild affects from the disease, but any cats that have been bred with both folded-ear parents are likely to suffer greatly. In these cats x-rays at as early as 7 weeks can determine the extent of the disease. This is why it is very important you do not buy a kitten from two folded-ear parents.

To ensure your cat is not suffering as it gets older, you can keep doing the tail test. Gently move the tail up and down and from side to side, if your cat is visibly in pain by this, it could be a sign of arthritis. To double-check you will need to take your cat to the veterinarian immediately.

Treating Osteochondrodysplasia

There is no full cure for the disease and in some cases surgery is recommended to make movement easier for your cat. If OCD develops very early your veterinarian may suggest euthanizing to prevent further suffering.

In some milder cases your veterinarian will prescribe a course of glucosamine and chondrotine sulphate, which will work to prevent further trauma to the joints.

2. Muscular Dystrophy

Muscular dystrophy is a genetic disorder that deteriorates the muscles of dogs and cats because of low amounts of dystrophin. It is this that causes the fold in some Scottish Fold's ears. Unfortunately, there is no a cure for the disease, but there are treatments available that can help slow down its progression.

The most common forms of muscular dystrophy begin at birth or shortly thereafter. While the condition is very serious, cats that survive to adulthood can often live fairly well as indoor companions for an average number of years (9-12 years).

In this disease, the muscles get weaker but they also get much larger. The tongue might get so large it pokes out of the mouth. There are other forms as well, some of which are most common in males, others in females.

Symptoms of muscular dystrophy

Most forms of muscular dystrophy appear very young, which is why you should look out for symptoms if adopting a kitten. These symptoms include:

- Troubles walking.
- Difficulties breathing, or eating.
- There could be vomiting
- A downward flexion of the head and neck.
- Kittens may also develop an odd posture and a hopping gait.
- Blood tests and a muscle biopsy confirm the diagnosis.

Treating muscular dystrophy

Unfortunately, there is no cure, and no established treatment can slow the progression of the disease. Steroids help some animals remain functional longer. There is also some promising research being done with stem cells.

For now, however, treatment focuses on supporting the kitten's general health and treating the symptoms rather than the disease itself, responding to any complications that arise. For example, if your cat has muscular dystrophy he/she is at very high risk of aspiration pneumonia, the result of inhaling saliva or food. You and your vet can work together to try to keep it from happening, and your vet can treat pneumonia if it does occur. Another possible complication is renal failure, however your vet can treat this too.

The disease can be very difficult for your cat and can be sad to witness in any pet. But if you work together with your veterinarian you should be able to control it and ensure your beloved Scottish Fold has the best life quality it can possibly get.

If you suspect your chosen kitten does have muscular dystrophy but you want to go ahead with your adoption you may face substantial veterinary costs. You may find it difficult to get a good insurance policy also, since it is a genetic condition. Talk to your vet and have them give you an average annual cost of caring for a cat with muscular dystrophy in its worst-case scenario. If you feel comfortable you can handle the costs then you should be able to give your Scottish Fold a good life. However, it is essential that your cat is spayed/neutered to prevent further breeding of the disease itself.

3. Hypertrophic Cardiomyopothy (HCM)

This form of heart disease has been spotted within Scottish Folds but it is unclear as yet if it is due to any genetic mutation. It is the most common acquired heart diseases in cats in general, however. It is a primary heart muscle disease where the muscular walls of the ventricles become abnormally thick (hypertrophied). The name hypertrophic cardiomyopathy literally means 'thick heart muscle disease'.

Similar to the same disease in humans, HCM is thought to inherit from a dominant gene. Many purebred cats are predisposed to the disease but the domestic short hair (regular house cat) is the type most commonly diagnosed with HCM. Since shorthairs are commonly used to breed with Scottish Folds, this could explain the prevalence within the breed. The disease usually occurs in middle aged to older cats however, the disease can be diagnosed at any age, often less than 5 years in purebred cats. Basically, HCM is not contracted through any kind of virus or nutritional deficiency but is entirely genetic. Therefore, other than test for it early on, there is nothing a pet owner can do to prevent the disease.

Symptoms of HCM

As an owner it is very difficult to spot any signs of HCM, a cat can go a lifetime with HCM and you wouldn't even know. Additionally, cats are masters at masking problems until they become severe, so cats with severe HCM may appear completely normal or have only subtle signs that go unnoticed. There are some small indications that your cat may suffer from HCM and these include:

- Faster breathing.
- A loss of appetite.
- If HCM is more severe you could notice clear respiratory distress
- Again, in severe cases there may be leg paralysis caused by a blood clot.

Your veterinarian will be able to give the best analysis and proper diagnosis when he or she listens to your cat's chest during their physical exam. Your vet will be looking out for symptoms such as an increased heart rate, heart murmur, and/or gallop rhythm (extra heart sound), which may be a clear sign as the disease advances.

If your vet suspects HCM your Scottish Fold may need an echocardiogram (ultrasound of the heart), which offers the best means to diagnose HCM. Echocardiography allows a veterinarian to observe the physical structure and dynamic function of the heart. This is a non invasive test, so you don't have to worry about causing your cat any distress

Sometimes additional tests might be needed to rule out underlying diseases such as systemic hypertension or hyperthyroidism which may cause similar hypertrophy of the left ventricle as HCM. If no other causes are found, the diagnosis of HCM is made.

In very extreme cases, HCM can lead to arrhythmias (abnormal heartbeat) and can result in sudden death this is similar to what is seen in young basketball and soccer players that suddenly die during a game. It is very difficult to predict which cats are likely to do this, but luckily sudden death is relatively uncommon in cats.

A small number of cats can suffer from feline aortic thromboembolism (FATE) – a blood clot in the aorta that causes blockage of blood flow to the back legs (most commonly), leading to sudden paralysis, severe pain, and often, death.

How is HCM Treated?

Unfortunately, there is currently no cure for HCM. The changes occurring to the heart muscle are irreversible. However, in some cases, the problems occurring with the left ventricle in your Scottish Fold's heart are due to another underlying heart disease, such as hyperthyroidism. Treating this primary disease could result in some or complete resolution of the heart condition.

Your veterinarian may prescribe one or more medications to try to improve the heart's relaxing ability if HCM is clear. However, it is important to mention that there have been no drugs that have been successful in doing this. Thus, attempts to reduce the risk of heart failure and to help the heart function efficiently are largely theoretical and may ultimately be of no value. It is quite acceptable to not treat cats with HCM prior to the onset of CHF but if new drugs become available this may change.

However, your veterinarian may wish to pursue some treatment options. Drugs that may be prescribed include:

- Drugs that are thought to encourage relaxation of heart muscle, or slow down the heart rate to allow a longer time for the heart to fill, or both. As mentioned, there is no evidence that either of these approaches actually benefits cats with HCM.

- Drugs to treat congestive heart failure (diuretics and ACE inhibitors). These medications are not specific for HCM, but are used in cats with heart failure secondary to any heart condition. With severe fluid build-up in the chest cavity, the veterinarian may physically remove the fluid with a catheter to help the cat breathe.

- Drugs that are thought to reduce the risk of clot formation, or clot recurrence. A medication that reduces the ability of the blood to clot may be prescribed if your cat is felt to be at risk for blood clot formation or currently has a blood clot in one of its arteries or heart chambers. The use of certain drugs for this purpose is closely monitored to insure the patient is not placed at risk of haemorrhages. Treatment does not guarantee that a blood clot will not form and it will not break down previously formed clots. Once again, there are no studies showing that any of these medications actually do what they're claimed to do.

As an owner of a cat with HCM, you should be very sensitive to changes in your pet's condition and should not hesitate to seek veterinary advice. Your veterinarian may show you how to monitor your cat's respiratory rate as an increased rate may be a sign that congestive heart failure is developing or worsening. Cats with congestive heart failure do not cough like dogs or people, but often exhibit open mouth breathing and panting. A cat that is having difficulty breathing from heart failure or has loss of function of hindlimbs or front limbs, requires veterinary care as quickly as possible. In the acute setting, these problems may need specific treatments (oxygen therapy, injectable medications, anticoagulation medications, or pain medications) that can only be offered by a veterinarian.

4. Polycystic kidney disease (PKD)

Polycystic Kidney Disease (PKD) is another inherited condition, which causes multiple cysts on the kidneys. The disease is most common in Persians and other exotic breeds but has been found to be fairly common with Scottish Folds. The cysts are present from birth, but start out small and slowly increasing in size. The cysts can range from very small to several centimeters in diameter. The increasing size of these cysts can damage the normal kidney tissue and in the worst cases, cause kidney failure.

Again, this is not a disease that is caught virally or through nutritional deficiencies. Genetic studies have shown that PKD in cats is autosomal (a non sex linked gene) dominant. This means only one parent needs the gene to pass it onto the offspring. There is a 50% chance of a cat inheriting PKD if a parent has it. If a cat is genetically free of PKD it is not possible to pass it onto offspring. If your Scottish Fold does have PKD, it is essential they be neutered to prevent the disease being passed on to further offspring.

Much like HCM, some cats may a go a lifetime with PKD and the owner will not be able to tell. However, generally speaking the lifespan of a cat with PKD is seven years. Some cats may suffer much earlier and some later, it varies from cat to cat.

Symptoms of PKD

As mentioned before, unless the cysts increase in size it is impossible for an owner to tell if their cat has PKD. As the cysts grow, however, the symptoms can become more apparent. These include:

- Lethargy.
- Weight loss.
- Vomiting.

The main symptom to look out for is polyuria and polydypisia. Polyuria means excessive urination and polydipsia is an excessive thirst caused by the dehydration. It is essential if you suspect PKD that you take your Scottish Fold to the veterinarian clinic straight away. By feeling your cat the vet will be able to see if the kidneys have grown in size and will run further tests to get a diagnosis.

If PKD is suspected, your veterinarian will run the following tests:

- **Ultrasound:** After 10 moths of age a veterinarian will be able to diagnose PKD with around 98% accuracy.
- **Genetic Test:** Even more accurate than the ultrasound. A genetic test is completed by taking a swab from inside your cat's cheek and then sent to a specialized laboratory for results. This test is 99.9% accurate.

How is PKD treated?

Unfortunately there is no way to slow down the growth of the cysts and they cannot be removed. As the kidneys begin to fail, they lose their ability to filter out toxins. Kidneys also help control blood pressure by releasing an enzyme called renin. When blood pressure drops and kidneys don't receive enough blood, renin is released; causing blood vessels to contract and when blood vessels contract, blood pressure goes up.

Therefore, veterinarians will take measures to treat the secondary causes of kidney failure. Helping reduce the level of toxins in the cat is important. Your veterinarian may administer fluids subcutaneously to treat the dehydration. Your cat may also require a particular prescription diet. This prescription diet will contain a lower percentage of protein and less phosphorus than normal cat food.

Cats obviously need protein every day for growth, building muscles and repairing tissue, as we have already touched upon. After the body uses the protein in the foods, a waste product called urea is made. Cats with kidney failure are not able to get rid of this urea normally. Damaged kidneys may not be able to remove phosphorus from the blood to and this causes the level of phosphorus in the blood to become too high. A high blood phosphorus level may cause the cat to lose calcium from their bones. To help stop this from happening phosphorus binders may be given. These come in tablet or capsule form. Antacids and anti nausea medication will help regulate the levels of acidity in your cat's blood stream from the food they consume.

Medication may also be prescribed if your cat's blood pressure is too high, this will give your cat the correct levels it needs and prevent any further complications.

Cats with kidney failure sometimes have a low red blood cell count too. Only the human form is available to administer and some cats may eventually recognize this substance as foreign and antibodies will be created against it.

Overall, treatment can vary from cat to cat. Treatment depends on the severity of the kidney failure, based on how large the cysts are and how fast they are growing. Again, cats with only a few small and slow growing cysts may never be diagnosed and live to a good age, eventually dying from something else. Although there is no cure there are steps that can be taken to help curb the affects of the disease.

5. Common problems with shorthaired cats

Scottish Folds are often bred with shorthaired cats such as the British and American Shorthairs. This means that they can possibly inherit some of their medical problems. The chances of this are less than the diseases listed above but still something you should watch out for.

6. Respiratory issues

Medically, troubled breathing is known as dyspnea while rapid and short breathing is known as tachypnea. These difficulties, if neglected, can become life threatening for your cat. Therefore, it is necessary to have your cat thoroughly diagnosed if you observe one or more of the conditions mentioned below.

Symptoms of respiratory issues

Symptoms can be hard to spot until the condition is more advanced, so keep an eye out for decreased mobility and the general signs you would expect from a cat that is struggling to breathe. The more specific symptoms include:

- Evident movement in the chest and belly while breathing
- Nostrils flare open
- The mouth is kept open to aid breathing
- The elbows stick out from the body while breathing
- The head and neck are stretched out in front of the body
- Breathing in is difficult
- Breathing is accompanied by loud noises
- Fast Breathing
- The mouth is open while breathing
- Breaths are short paced and shallow
- The pace is really high

It is also common for cats to cough excessively when they have breathing difficulties. The treatment of breathing disorders is based on the causes of the problems. Here are some common causes of breathing issues.

Troubled Breathing

- Deformed nostrils
- Tumors or Infections in the nose, chest or mouth
- Elongated palate
- Allergic reaction
- Fluid accumulation in the lungs
- Toxins in the chest due to botulism
- Bloating of the stomach
- Blood accumulation in the chest region
-

Rapid Breathing

- Reduced levels of Oxygen in the Blood
- Anemia
- Asthma
- Accumulation of fluids in the lungs
- Accumulation of fluids in the area around the lungs
- Bleeding in the lungs
- Tumors

Diagnosis of Breathing Difficulties

Since the breathing difficulties in your Scottish Fold cat may have several reasons ranging from tumors to infections, the need to diagnose the condition thoroughly is high. You must make sure that you leave no stones unturned in discovering the cause for breathlessness in the cat. Negligence in this area may have fatal consequences.

A diagnosis always begins with a background study of the cat to determine the incidents that may have preceded the condition. Diagnosis includes observation of the breathing patterns of the cat. The presence of heart murmurs is checked by listening to the chest. The color of the gums plays an important role in determining the reason for breathlessness. If the supply of oxygen is inadequate, the gums develop a bluish tinge.

There are some standard tests to determine the causes and symptoms of breathlessness in your cat. They include:

- Blood count
- Biochemical profile
- Urine analysis
- Blood test

These tests are useful in understanding if your cat is suffering from a low blood cell count. The presence of any internal infection can also be determined using these tests. The severity of the breathing disorder can be determined using these tests.

Other tools used to diagnose breathing difficulties are ultrasound and x ray imaging. This is used to check the structure of the abdomen. In case there is a possibility of a heart disorder, your vet may recommend an ECG as well. Endoscopy is a common tool used to determine causes related to the airways or the nose.

Treatment of Breathing Disorders

The treatment depends entirely upon the cause for the breathing difficulty in your cat. In most cases, it is necessary to admit your cat to a hospital or a proper facility to provide the required amount of oxygen. Medication will be provided orally or intravenously to help the cat breathe better. Activity of the cat might be restricted until he has recovered completely.

Precautions to be taken

Cage rest might be recommended for your Scottish Fold to get enough rest. Make sure you follow all the instructions given by your veterinarian. In case you observe any relapse in the breathing pattern, consult your doctor immediately.

7. Watery eyes in your Scottish Fold

Cats, unlike humans, never cry. So, in case your cat has extremely teary or watery eyes, do not assume that it is some form of emotional outburst. This condition means that your pet is in need of medical attention.

The abnormal flow of tears is also known as epiphora. This is a common condition in several breeds of cats and has been associated with distinct shapes of eyes. Sometimes, there are conditions like the turning in of eyelashes or eyelids that can be observed right from the time your Scottish Fold was born. In short haired cats the absence of eyelids is also a common observation. This leads to eye irritation and watering in the Scottish Fold cat.

Symptoms of Epiphora

The common symptoms of Epiphora include:

- Tear drainage
- Tear stains on the face
- Formation of ulcers in the cornea
- Sagging of the skin around the eye
- Regular discharge from the eye
- Irritation and redness in the eyes
- Inflammation in the eyes
- Constant squinting

If the condition is congenital i.e. by birth, there are chances that the opening of the eyelid is abnormally large. This leads to too much exposure of the eyeball, causing continuous watering. In case of eyelid tumors, you will be able to see a very evident patch of skin on the eyelids. Although this condition is very rare in the Scottish Fold, it is something you must keep an eye out for.

Causes of Epiphora

Watery eyes in cats are usually linked to other conditions that your Scottish Fold has acquired. They include:

- Fracture of the facial bones
- Swelling in the area adjacent to the tear drainage system
- Tumors in the eyelids
- Infections of tumors in the nasal cavity, eyelids and the eye
- Any blockage or inflammation of the tear duct can cause inflammation and overflow of tears
- Lack of normal openings in the tear drainage system can cause watery eyes. This is a congenital condition.

- Presence of extra openings in the tear drainage system can also lead to watery eyes.
- In case there is an absence of openings between the tear drainage system and the nose, excessive tear formation is observed.
- Inflammation of the eyes

Glaucoma is also prevalent in some cats with teary eyes. In case of glaucoma, the internal pressure of the eye increases tremendously, leading to the formation of tears.

Any disorder in the eye or the cornea leads to watering of the eyes. Sometimes, there is also a fair chance that your Scottish Fold has developed infections when you took him out for a walk or just let him out of the door.

Diagnosis of Epiphora

In order to understand the possible causes of epiphora, your vet might request for a background check of your cat's activities before proceeding into actual diagnosis. It is absolutely mandatory to diagnose the causes for watery eyes thoroughly.

Radiographs are very useful in checking for lesions in the nasal cavity and sinus area. Sometimes, a contrast material is used to understand the different structures that might be present. Your vet may also recommend magnetic resonance imaging or computed tomography to get a clearer picture of what is leading to the watery eyes.

For laboratory analysis, the material produced inside the cat's eye is taken and tested. Sometimes, when your vet is unable to arrive at any conclusive diagnosis, he might recommend surgical examination.

If the suspected cause is a foreign body, there are two methods of diagnosis. The first one involves flushing the tear duct. The second one is the use of a fluorescent stain to check for foreign objects under a blue light. Once the condition has been discovered, suitable treatment options are recommended for your kitty.

Treatment of Epiphora

There are a number of factors that need to be addressed when treating Epiphora which your veterinarian will be able to talk you through:

- The most important step in the treatment of epiphora is the reduction of irritation in the cat's eyes. This can be achieved by washing the foreign bodies out from the tissues of the eye.
- In case of any primary eye disease like corneal ulcers and conjunctivitis, treating them will become priority.
- Lesions that are blocking the tear duct must be managed to allow the normal flow of tears.
- If the cause for tear formation is any physical abnormality in the eyelid, surgery is recommended. These procedures are quite straightforward and only involve tacking the lids into the required position.
- If the eyelashes are a problem, they are removed by cryosurgery.
- If tumors are present, they are treated quite aggressively. The primary fear with tumors is that they may spread into other areas in the head including the optic nerve and the brain.

Medications are suggested based on the causes for watering. These medicines range from pain killers to antibiotic ointment depending upon the assistance your cat needs to speed up the healing process.

Precautions to take if your cat has Epiphora

The recovery phase is very important. Even a little bit of negligence can result in a relapse of irritation and inflammation. It is recommended that you use an Elizabethan collar during the healing phase. In case of inflammation, your vet might ask you to bring your cat for reevaluation once in seven days till the condition is completely fixed. If the problem persists, then you might have to improve the diagnosis efforts.

When surgical procedures have been performed, you must ensure that the dressing is checked regularly along with proper medication and cleaning. You must take your cat for regular checkups to ensure that there is no recurrence or relapse of the condition. Also, surgical procedures are subject to the risk of infections. So proper management of the wound and revaluation is an important part of the recovery phase.

Chapter 14: Is Your Scottish Fold Obese?

Scottish Fold cats usually weigh up to 9-12 lbs /4-6kg in their adulthood. They are fairly relaxed cats who may not get as much exercise as other cats. Also if they suffer from any health problems common to their breed as we have already discussed, they may find moving around a struggle. On top of this, like most cats, they love their food. So, if you do not take good care of their diet, there are chances your Scottish Fold will become obese or overweight.

A plump kitty may sound nice and cute. But, in case of medium sized cats like the Scottish Fold, the effect that they have on his health and wellbeing are always negative. Besides usual problems like sluggishness and lethargy, obesity in cats has several associated health disorders.

Scottish Fold cats are also largely indoor cats. This means that they need constant stimulation to keep themselves active. If your cat is unable to get the amount of exercise that he/she requires, be prepared to deal with 'weighty' kitty issues.

1. How to tell if your cat is obese

Sometimes, it becomes very difficult to determine if your cat is, indeed, overweight. The level of activity and the agility seems to be just fine. So, cat owners think that they have a happy and fat kitty. But, there are surefire ways of telling if your cat is becoming obese. You can try three simple tests at home before you have an actual expert test your cat for obesity:

- Feel the area around the rib cage of your cat. If you are still able to feel the rib cage through his fur, it means that he is still not obese. However if you have to press really hard to get to his rib cage, it means that your cat is heavier than the normal, acceptable weight.

- There is a distinct shape in a cat's waistline. The body tapers from the belly towards the hind quarters. If it is too stubby and even, it is a sign that your cat needs to lose weight.
- A hanging pouch between the hind legs of a cat is a definite indication of the cat being overweight.

Like humans, cats that are overweight will experience several health issues. Therefore, you must take necessary measures to slim down your cat and maintain a healthy weight.

2. Health disorders in overweight cats

One of the most common complaints in veterinary clinics across the globe is health disorders related to obesity. The biggest threat to the well being of cats is feline diabetes mellitus. The second most prevalent disorder in cats due to obesity is hyperthyroidism, which is due to excessive production of thyroid.

According to experts, the chances of an obese cat becoming diabetic are double in comparison to cats that have a normal weight. This risk becomes 8 times if the cat becomes severely obese. The association between obesity and diabetes is quite evident. When your cat becomes obese, there is a drastic increase in the amount of inflammatory markers and oxidative stress. This causes insulin resistance, which leads to obesity.

The resistance to insulin is one of the most common problems found in cats. It has also been observed, that a change in the diet is not as effective in increasing insulin sensitivity as the actual reduction in weight.
There are several other health conditions that can be found in cats due to feline obesity:

- Osteoarthritis and lameness- This condition occurs because there is too much stress on the medium sized frame of your cat. You will be able to hear loud thuds

when your cat jumps off a table or chair, which indicates a
gradual loss of agility in the cat.
- There are several skin problems like dermatoses, as the cat
is not able to groom himself properly. He is not agile
enough to reach out to all the spots on his body.
- Too much pressure on the liver also causes liver problems
like feline lipidosis syndrome.
- Urinary tract disorders are common in cats who are obese.

The biggest issue with obesity is not the condition itself. The
inability of many owners to recognize this condition and provide
necessary treatment is the cause for the drastic increase in feline
obesity in the last couple of years. There are many cases that have
been reported where owners are just used to over-feeding their
cat. They actually find a normal sized cat malnourished and
unhealthy.
As the owner, it is your responsibility to evaluate the condition of
your cat's body on a regular basis. You can also get a body
condition score to check for the amount of fat present in your
cat's body. These scores show the difference in the calorie intake
of your cat and the actual energy requirement. If your cat is being
overfed, the score will increase to indicate an increase in fat
deposits.

3. Tackling obesity in cats

It is not very difficult to maintain the normal body weight. All
you need to do is ensure that the width of the hips and shoulders
are maintained without any visible bulge on the sides. You must
also make sure that the belly of your cat does not hang too low.

There are a few things you can do to reduce obesity in your cat:

Understand what the right amount of food is

The amount of food that you give your cat should be just enough
to keep them healthy. It is impossible to put a number on the

amount of food that you can give your Scottish Fold. However, you can measure the calorie intake in your cat. He will require about 55 kilocalories per kilo of body weight. So, in case of the average Scottish Fold, they will need close to 250 kilocalories each day.

Depending on your cat's health, you can determine how much food he requires. If there has been any recent surgical procedure or neutering, you must make sure you reduce the food intake accordingly. Free choice feeding is a very common problem among cat owners. They provide their cat with a range of flavors and choices leading to over eating. If you mix dry cat food with canned food, there might be chances of overeating. Constant change in the taste makes your cat overeat because of novel tastes that he is able to experience.

Use a measuring cup to ensure that your cat is neither over fed, nor under fed. If you prefer free choice feeding, divide the food into two portions. Give your cat one helping in the morning and one in the evening. You must also be very careful that the feeding is age appropriate. Depending on whether you have a kitten or a senior cat in your household, the choice of diet will vary.

Keep your Cat Hydrated

You must make sure that there is plenty of fresh water available for your cat, especially if you are feeding him dry cat food. While most dry foods work very well for cats, lack of water might lead to issues like urinary tract disorders and also lowered kidney function.

Water is an essential nutrient for your cat. Irrespective of whether you are feeding him wet or dry food, you must give him enough water. The presence of adequate amounts of water in the body will help your cat assimilate the food that he has consumed. Proper digestion and elimination, which is the key to good health in a cat, is regulated by the amount of water available.

Give your Cat a Low Fat Diet

For an indoor cat, like the Scottish Fold, who is not very active, a low fat diet is mandatory. If you have put your cat on a weight loss diet, you must give him adequate amounts of protein. It is true that the calorie intake must be restricted. However, you must always make sure that you do not reduce the amount of essential nutrients. When you increase the amount of proteins, weight loss is aided while keeping the lean body mass intact.

Keep a Check on the treats

If you are concerned about the health of your cat, make sure you reduce the amount of treats and tidbits. This practice must be extended to at least a couple of weeks after the 'diet' period. You must make sure that everyone in your family is aware of this rule. If you try and cheat out of affection, remember that you are harming your cat's health. It would help, instead, to cut your cat's meal down to smaller, more frequent meals. This will ensure that he does not experience hunger pangs while continuing to stay on a healthy diet.

Say No to Crash Diets

Crash diets are harmful for cats and they are harmful for humans. You must never starve your cat. In fact, no matter what restrictions you make in his diet, it must be supervised by a dietician. If you do not keep a tab on the amount of minerals and vitamins your cat is getting, it can lead to a fatal condition called hepatic lipidosis, which affects the liver.

Keep the Activity Levels High

Exercise is extremely important in cats. You cannot control the health and weight of your cat by merely altering the diet. You must ensure that he has an active lifestyle. While controlling the calories he takes in, you must also make sure that he burns the calories through exercise and activity. Here are some things you must do to keep make your cat's environment stimulating and engaging:

- Set aside a dedicated time to play with your cats. You can use simple toys like strings to help your kitty play and get a good workout.

- Allow his natural instincts to take over. You must let your cat climb, scratch and even chase around the house. These exercises are interesting to him, by nature, and will increase the process of weight loss.

- Get a feeding ball to give your cat one meal in the day. The advantage with the feeding ball is that your cat will have to put in some amount of effort to roll the ball and get to the food inside.

- The food bowl of your cat can be placed on top of a flight of stairs. This will encourage him to climb to get to the food.

- Try to take your cat outdoors as often as possible. A breath of fresh air will do you and your kitty a great deal of good.

Throughout the process of weight loss, you must be extremely patient. It will take several weeks and even months for your cat to lose weight. If you find it too hard to maintain the weight of your cat on your own, you can ask your vet for tips. You can even enroll in a veterinary weight loss clinic for additional support and information.

Chapter 15: Getting Your Cat Spayed/Neutered

1. Why get your Scottish Fold cat spayed?

The obvious reason to get your cat spayed or neutered is for your own peace of mind; knowing there is no chance of an unexpected litter coming in to your household. However, the benefits of having your cat neutered bring even more advantages than just this. Female cats who are spayed are less likely to develop ovarian and breast cancers and neutered males are less likely to develop testicular cancer. Neutering male cats particularly prevents the spread of venereal disease and they are less likely to suffer injuries as intact males have a natural instinct to roam and get in to fights.

Perhaps one of the most important consequences of getting your cat spayed is that you will be preventing further overpopulation of cats. Even an indoor cat may escape and produce kittens if not sterilized. Each year, millions more homeless cats are euthanized or end up in shelters due to a lack of good homes. Therefore any assistance from cat-owners to control the population is greatly needed.

2. What happens when your cat is spayed/neutered?

Check with your vet for the pre-operative care involved with your cat to have them spayed. If your cat is older they may ask you not to feed them in the twelve hours leading up to the procedure. During the operation your cat will undergo a general anesthetic and for female cats the vet will remove the ovaries, fallopian tubes and the uterus.

In the days following the procedure you may notice your cat will be more subdued and may have less of an appetite, however this should pass soon enough. There is a myth that says sterilized cats become different cats and end up being lazy and putting on weight. This is most certainly not the case; your cat's personality will remain the same given a few days to recover. You may be given pain medication to take home with you, which your vet will explain. Back at home make sure your cat is given a quiet space to relax and recover in, preferably away from other animals. Try to prevent them from over-exerting themselves, however they will not be over eager to jump around straight away so you should not have to restrict them too much. It is essential they do not lick the incision as this may cause an infection. You may also wish to change your litter to something softer, such as shredded paper, as normal litter can sometimes irritate and cause infection. With plenty of TLC and some care put in to their recovery your beloved Scottish Fold will be back to it's normal, loving self in no time!

3. Possible complications

As with any operation there may be some complications with spaying a cat. Sometimes they may suffer hernias or internal bleeding if the blood vessels were not adequately tied off. However these complications are rare and should by no means deter you from spaying your cat.

If you notice any unusual swelling or think your cat is in pain take them back to the vets immediately and they will check over the incision and ensure there have not been any problems. Infections can easily be avoided as long as your cat does not lick the incision, if they do continue to do so you can buy a cat collar for them to wear while the incision heals.

Chapter 16: Behavioral Problems And How To Deal With Them.

1. Possible behavioral problems common with cats

It is rare that a Scottish Fold will be mischievous. Although they are a fairly active cat, they are never boisterous and their eagerness to please you will mean they will rarely give you cause to worry. However, no cat is perfect and even the Scottish Fold may have some behavioral problems from time to time. Often the causes for this are easily solvable and hopefully, it never becomes too much of a problem and simply adds to their personality. Saying this, cats are notoriously reluctant to be trained so the smaller problems may become little nuances that you just have to deal with as a cat owner.

In some cases, behavioral problems in cats can be detrimental to your home and other animals. If bad behavior occurs when they are kittens it is a lot simpler to eradicate. However, if your cat suddenly starts exhibiting bad behavior ask yourself what may have changed to cause this. Usual reasons for sudden changes in behavior are anxiety, loneliness, stress, loss of a companion, illness, problems with other cats and boredom. Whatever the cause bad or harmful behavior needs to be stopped immediately before it becomes a habit, at which point your task will be a lot more difficult. Below are some of the problems that some cat owners have suffered with and some simple solutions that should help stop the behavior being repeated.

Aggressiveness: If this occurs continuously in male cats the best and most effective solution is sterilization. There is a theory that aggressive behavior arises from additives in food. Try switching to organic food, which may stop the problem. When kittens are acting aggressively or over excited a good trick is to lay a blanket over them for a short time to calm them down.

Aggression directed at human beings: It is unlikely that cats become friendly with everybody who visits your home. But, most of the domesticated cats are civil to guests and will simply disappear from the scene if they are uncomfortable in the surroundings. However, when a cat tends to get aggressive towards people in general, it is a clear indication of the fact that the particular cat has been poorly trained when it was younger. Biting, scratching and unpleasant vocalization are indications of a badly trained cat. Some other causes of aggressive cat behavior towards human beings are listed below:

- **Overstimulation:** This problem surfaces when the owner of the cat does not understand the body language of the cat. There are cats that prefer petting while most prefer to be left alone. Even the most petting friendly cats do not like to be petted for unreasonable lengths of time. When they get over stimulated, they tend to scratch or bite to show that their petting session is over. If one closely observes, then, he/she will see that the cat starts pulling himself away, by pulling his ears back and by narrowing his eyes. If the owner fails to understand these signals, then, the cat begins to lash its tail. At the end, when the owner is simply being ignorant, then the aggression sets in.

- **Redirected aggression:** A cat's aggression towards her owner or other human beings may not necessarily be due to patting; sometimes, the sight of something disturbing can also result in aggression. When your cat spots a foreign cat or any other stranger animal around the house, then there is a possibility of the cat getting irritated by the sight itself. As a reaction to this, your cat will scratch or bite the first thing it can reach.

- **Medical causes:** This sort of behavior can also be a result of internal, undetected injuries or any other medical causes. This can range from hormonal imbalance to flea infestation. The cat expresses its distress through either biting or clawing dangerously.

Soiling accidents: If soiling occurs with an older cat that you have had for a while it is normally a sign of illness. If this is the case take your cat to the vets to run some tests and investigate it further. If your cat is not ill try pinpointing the problem. Is there something off-putting about the litter tray? Have you switched to new litter? Have you recently moved? Is the house less peaceful? Where possible, litter trays need to be in a quiet space and as private as they can be. The tray must always be accessible and frequently cleaned out.

Spraying: When a cat sprays it is marking its territory. This is common in a multi-cat household; it is also common for cats to spray on their owner's legs as a sign of affection. If a cat sprays in more then one place this could be a sign of anxiety and so try to pinpoint when it started happening and identify the route causes. If there is one specific area that your cat sprays make sure you clean the area thoroughly rendering the act useless. Converting the sprayed area in to a play space will also help deter future sprays. This way the area has a new purpose and the cat would not want to spray there. Again, if this suddenly occurs with older cats and there have been no identifiable changes it is best to take your cat to the vet who may be able to identify a health problem.

Scratching: Unfortunately, scratching is not only ubiquitous with cat ownership but it is also a completely natural urge and rarely as a consequence from any changes. Usually a cat has a favorite sofa or chair it tends to scratch but if it occurs throughout your home this could be a sign of anxiety. The best method to combatting this is to purchase a scratching post. Whenever you see your cat about to scratch a piece of furniture or carpet, move them to the scratching post. If possible place the post near the place they scratch most. When they go to the post as opposed to your favorite armchair, praise them and play with them a little.

Overgrooming: This is not necessarily a destructive trait to you as an owner but if left untreated overgrooming can result in hair loss and infections for your cat. If the overgrooming is a cause of a skin infection diagnosed by a vet the best way to fight it is to buy a cat collar until the infection has passed. However, if there is no original infection overgrooming is usually due to a mental problem such as OCD, anxiety, boredom, stress or conflict. Firstly, if you can identify the cause do so and try to resolve it. There could be an outside cat, they may have lost their sleeping spot or are having conflicts with other pets. When trying to stop overgrooming distract your cat when they do it by making loud noises and initiating play. When they do stop grooming lavish praise on them and give them plenty of attention.

Attention Seeking Disorder: Cats are known to 'meow' nonstop at certain times of the day or night, but the Scottish Fold is a quiet cat that you will rarely hear a peep out of. But in rare cases some cats may meow or moan excessively and this can become a nuisance for the owner. When concerning the Scottish Fold especially it is sensible to sit down and understand what is causing your cat to behave in this particular manner. Since Scottish Folds are quiet, there could be something wrong causing the sudden chattiness. Howling of your cat can be broadly categorized as either crying or meowing. The cause for such behavior can be either emotional or physical pain that the cat is experiencing. Experts have noted that the attention seeking demeanor of the cats can be further classified as follows:

- **Mournful howl:** Some cats tend to howl in the night like they are calling out for help. This particular howl can make the cat owner cringe with sympathy for the poor creature. This mournful howl is mostly a result of deafness. In some cases this cry has been identified as the cat's cry for help in its old age. It is also associated with the insanity of an old cat. The reason for this howl need not always be an emotional one. A certain condition called as Feline hyperesthesia is also associated with this behavior. When a cat howls during the night and is found to roll around in the house, you must consider this condition. This condition is commonly called Rippling

Skin Disorder. This disorder is considered a stress disorder. However, the symptoms usually include a set of unrelated issues. The cats tend to become extremely sensitive to touch and the skin begins to show ripples. The possible causes of this disorder are: excessive presence of unsaturated fatty acids in combination with Vitamin E deficiency, brain infection or trauma or flea allergies. If the cat is diagnosed with this disorder then it is unlikely that it will be completely cured. So, paying attention to these issues can help you provide greater comfort to the cat and keep tabs on its behavioral issue.

- **Chronic pseudo hunger:** Hunger pangs are commonly observed in cats as well. Like human beings, cats also have food cravings that are unwarranted. Cats tend to develop a lot of liking towards some treats such as tuna flakes. This can also turn into an addiction of sorts. When you observe that your cat has been begging for food all day the reason is not hunger but pseudo hunger.

- **The figure 8:** Cats are known to run around their owner's feet in circles. This is also categorized under attention seeking issues of the cat. They are much like kids who need a little bit of extra attention. They also tend to rub themselves against your arm when they need extra attention.

- **Meow chat:** Cats are very vocal. They also like to have conversations with their owners. And, some chatty cats tend to prod their owners into lengthy conversations. If the owner refuses to spend enough time with the cat, then it tends to suffer from excessive loneliness.

2. How to restrain a cat

In exceptional circumstance you may need to restrain your cat. This may be due to aggressive behavior or the need to give them an injection at the vet. There are a number of techniques that you can use but we recommend to be careful when trying them and consult your veterinarian first.

If your cat is being overly aggressive you need to be very careful. The primary cause for aggression in a cat is fear; this may have been ignited by another animal or could have been a reaction to the veterinary surgery. In this case there are a number of techniques you can try. One simple calming technique is to look your cat in the eye and blink slowly but without closing your eyes completely, this is known as a 'calming-signal'.

Although scruffing is an effective technique to restraining a cat, this should be a last resort as this is potentially painful and not effective in the long run. An alternative and much more calming approach is to place three fingers on the top of their head with your thumb and pinky fingers at the base of their ears. You can also try wrapping them in a blanket or towel, both calming them and restricting any aggressive movements.

If you do have to scruff your cat seek advice from your vet as they have been trained to do it properly and as painlessly as possible.

Can you train a cat?

Contrary to popular belief, cats can be trained. However, this is easier in some breeds more so than others. Scottish Folds are intelligent cats but they are also not as playful as some other breeds, so forcing them to do an activity may be hard. Another difficulty with training any cat comes in their lack of eagerness to please. Unlike dogs they will not respond to coercion and will never respond positively to punishment. The best way to get the results you want are to reward good behavior, train before dinner time, keep training sessions short and be consistent.

The more intelligent your cat is the easier you will find it to train them. A good trick for finding out how intelligent your Scottish Fold is, is to do the 'hoop test'. Take a hula-hoop, around 60cm in diameter and hold it 30cm above the ground. Hold a treat on one side of the hoop and try to get your cat to jump through the hoop in order to reach it. If it takes fewer than 28 times for your cat to figure this out then you have an intelligent Scottish Fold! At about 40-48 times your cat is about average and above 60 is bellow average intelligence.

Chapter 17: Breeding and Pregnancy

Due to the health problems so prevalent in the Scottish Fold breed, you have to be careful if you decide to breed them. It is strongly recommended that if you have a Scottish Fold with the folded ears that you do not breed at all. This is because you risk breeding kittens with osteochonrodysplasia, as we have discussed already. This becomes almost a certainty if you breed two Scottish Folds together, if one of them has the folded ears. However, if your Scottish Fold does not have the folded ears the chances of passing on the disease greatly decrease. Just to be safe it is better to breed with an American or British shorthair, in breeding trials these breeds have been found to stabilize the Scottish Fold.

It is also worth noting that if your Scottish Fold is pedigree, it may be part of your agreement with your breeder that your cat is neutered or spayed, to prevent any further breeding. This is fairly common practice as breeders seek to protect their own business.

1. Reaching puberty

When a male cat reaches puberty, he is known as a Tom. On the other hand, a female cat that hits puberty is known as the queen. Puberty in male cats sets in when they are about 6 or 9 months old. Breeding a male cat is only a good idea if the litter that he came from was healthy and was of a good size. His mother should not have had any complications while giving birth. You can ask your breeder for this information before you buy your cat.
The female cat will experience multiple cycles of heat during the breeding season. This season usually starts in January or February and continues until October or November. The temperature during this season and the ration between light and dark hours will play a significant role in your cat's eat cycle.

A female cat is ready to bear kittens at the age of 7 to 9 months. She will remain fertile for at least 9 years after she hits puberty.

Only if your female cat comes from a healthy litter and a healthy mother should you consider breeding as a good option. You can have your cat tested for the possibility of genetic disorders and illnesses to understand how safe or reasonable it is to choose the option of breeding.

Most female cats will show obvious signs before the actual heat sets in. You will see her roll around on the floor, rub her against objects and also meow persistently. However, she will not allow a tom to mount her. This is not a sign of pain, as most owners presume. It is just your cat's hormones raging!

This heat cycle should last for about 8 days. The interval between one heat cycle and another is usually about 10 days. So expect your cat to exhibit this behavior at least twice in a month during the breeding season.
The hormonal changes that take place in the cat's body in this period are tremendous. While estrogen causes the onset of the heat cycle, progesterone takes over when she is pregnant. As the level of estrogen increases, the heat cycle will intensify. Once the level of estrogen drops, the heat cycle ends. This rise and fall of estrogen will only end when she is mated.

2. Finding the right mate

Cats are extremely sensitive creatures. Most often, they will be able to choose their own mates when you take them to the breeder. If your cat has not been neutered or spayed, make sure you take them to a good breeder, especially with a pedigree like the Scottish Fold.

You must always take a queen to the tom for breeding as she will not be too sensitive to these environmental changes during the mating process. The actual mating does not last for more than 4 minutes. Once this is over, the queen will break free by striking the male with her paw and turning away. The after reaction of the female is just cleaning herself after rolling a thrashing for a while. The after reaction may last up to 9 minutes.

If you are interested in producing a litter, you may have to allow your cat to be mated multiple times. With a single mating, there are only 50% chances of your cat getting pregnant. Studies show that female cats will allow up to 30 matings at intervals of 5 minutes.

One interesting fact about cats in general is that while each kitten has one father, the fathers of the kittens in a single litter may not have the same father. This is true because of the multiple mating processes. As a result, your litter may have several varieties of kitten, depending upon the cats that your queen has mated with.

3. How to tell if your Scottish Fold cat might be pregnant

From 4 months old a female cat can get pregnant and on average they carry litters of around three to five kittens. The pregnancy lasts nine weeks and obviously if you suspect she may be pregnant, the best way to check is to take your cat to the vet. Although there are some things you can look out for yourself. First and foremost you will notice your cat's personality will change. For Scottish Folds it may be hard to tell as they are usually so affectionate and calm anyway! They will act similarly to when they are in heat but with even more rolling around and meowing. Since they know they are carrying special cargo now they will take fewer risks and not over exert themselves unless they have to.

Within the first month of pregnancy there may be morning sickness and their appetite will change. This could mean they will eat much less or become ravenous, it depends on the cat. If your cat goes 48 hours without eating take them to the vet. As time goes on your cat could also begin nesting, finding a quiet and secluded spot and making it comfortable to give birth. You may also notice physical changes such as pink, enlarged nipples, which may secrete a milky substance. The physical changes could just be signs they are on heat, so look for other clues and if they all point towards pregnancy take them to your vet. If you want to make doubly sure you can purchase cat pregnancy tests, however these tend to be expensive and you would have to draw the blood yourself. It is often much more economic and effective to simply visit your vet.

It is important you take your cat to the vets for thorough examinations. They are trained to feel for embryos and ensure they are developing properly and without threat to the mother. They will also be able to tell you how many kittens your cat is expecting, this is vital information so you know what to anticipate during the delivery. A vet can usually tell if your cat is pregnant 20 days in to the pregnancy.

4. How to care for a pregnant cat

Generally speaking pregnant cats will care for themselves. As previously mentioned, they will not over exert themselves or put themselves in any direct danger. However, it is important you make this easy for them to do. So keep them away from other pets and children, this prevents potential aggression and the spread of infectious diseases.

In the last two weeks of pregnancy they will want to start preparing a maternity bed. You can make one yourself out of a cardboard box. Ensuring there are three high sides with one side about 10cm from the ground. There will need to be plenty of padding and space for the mother and her litter, use cushions and blankets that you have around the house so they have a scent of home. Unfortunately, as fussy as all cats are, they may reject your bed and want to make their own choice. You must allow her to do this so she has everything as she wants it for when the day comes. Once she has settled on a spot try and make the whole room or area as comfortable and quiet as possible; keep other pets away from her and do not try encourage her to play at any point. The kittens will need to be warm so ensure the area is kept at a minimum of 22°C. Once your cat is comfortable allow her to get used to the bed and the area, do not try to move her at any point.

As can be expected, sometimes there are problems with pregnancy so make sure you observe the mother and recognize anything unusual. Signs that there may be something wrong include the mother going off her food, being visibly distressed and crying and abnormal or foul smelling discharge. The mother's appetite may drop a little so if she seems visibly fine otherwise this is perfectly normal. If you recognize any of these signs be sure to take her to the vet immediately.

5. What to do during labor

Your vet will be able to explain the labor and answer any questions you may have so you are prepared for when the day comes. However, if at any point you suspect that something is wrong call your vet, this cannot be reiterated enough.

In the first stage of labor your cat will be experiencing contractions. She may pace around the room or have failed trips to the litter tray. When she is ready she will settle in her maternity bed. This may not be the bed that was planned but wherever she settles do no try to move her, unless she lies in a spot that will be too difficult for you to reach, such as under the bed or a the back of a dark closet. If this is the case be very careful and try not to move her too far. A good technique is to slide a blanket or towel underneath her and then move the towel with her on top as opposed to directly moving her body.

During labor you will need plenty of clean towels and cloths, a bowl of warm water, disposable gloves, dental floss and petroleum jelly. Your vet will supply you with either iodine or chlorexidine for the umbilical cord, make sure you know exactly what to do with it upon instructions from your vet and have it close to hand. It is also wise to ensure you have your vet's phone number to the ready and your cat carrier lined with a towel and ready to go should you need to.

Generally speaking kittens should arrive at a 30-45 minute interval but the gap could last up to an hour also. If no kittens have been born after 3-4 hours of labor there may be a problem so notify your vet. Additionally if the gap in between kittens is longer than 30 minutes and the mother is visibly straining this may also be a sign of complications.

Kittens can be born head first or feet first; either way is perfectly normal. Once a kitten is born the mother cat should break the amniotic sack, although she may be overtired at which point you need to step in. Holding a towel gently tear open the sack and clean the kitten's mouth to assist in their breathing, never use a sharp object to tear the sack. Then leave for the mother to clean the kitten thoroughly. Again, if the mother is unable to clean properly you can step in to help. Using a cloth gently clean the kitten's face and nose to remove the membranes. To dry take a warm cloth and move against the grain of their hair and gently rub to warm the kitten and encourage them to take their first breath.

The umbilical cord is usually bitten and subsequently broken by the mother also. However, if they are unable to do so or they are biting too close to the kitten you may need to step in. Cutting the cord too close to the kitten's body may cause infection or death. Take the dental floss and tie at least two inches away from the kitten, then tie again another inch down the cord and cut in between the two ties. Be sure to have clean hands or wear the disposable gloves. After it has been cut you can dip the chord in the iodine or chlorexidine, again, ensure you are clear on how to do this upon the advice from you vet.

When a kitten is born this should be shortly followed by a placenta; there should be an equal number of placentas and kittens. So, if a kitten has been born without a placenta to follow this may be a sign of a retained placenta and you should notify the vet. Some cats will eat the placenta as it is a good source of nutrients and will build their strength for the following kittens, but this is not essential and you can remove the after birth if they show no interest in doing this.

The whole labor can last up to 24 hours and the mother will need plenty of time to clean and feed her litter once it is over. For some cats they may show no interest in doing this, this is quite common the older the cat is and the more litters they have given birth to. If this is the case consult your vet immediately, do not handle the kittens unless it is essential for their own wellbeing.

6. How to care for newborn kittens

Much with the pregnancy and labor, you may find, as an owner, you do not have to do too much in the first few weeks of your kittens' lives. However, you may have adopted a newborn kitten that has been separated from their mother or the mother is not producing enough milk to keep all kittens in her litter well nourished. There is another scenario that we have already touched on briefly, some cats may reject their young and so caring for them will remain up to you.

To start with, a kitten needs nourishment, warmth and socialization. They will also need to learn to excrete by themselves. As has already been mentioned, the mother cat should be able to take care of all of these and all you will have to do is sit back and watch. However if your kitten was separated from their mother get in touch with your vet or local animal shelter. They may be able to let you know of another mother cat that your kitten would be able to feed of. If this is not an option you will need to consult your vet as to the best practice and milk replacement. You may need to use a syringe if the kitten is very young and this is best shown through face-to-face teaching form an experienced professional. After around 3 to 4 weeks you can start weaning them off their milk diet by introducing dry food in to their milk. Warm some of the milk replacement and serve in a shallow bowl with some dry food in it to soften it up.

Kittens need to be fed much more frequently than adult cats. Newborns will need milk every 1 to 2 hours. At 3 or 4 weeks they will need feeding five times a day and after 6 months they can go down to three times a day.

Other than nourishment it is essential that kittens are kept warm during the first few weeks after birth. A simple home technique is to take a hot water bottle and wrap a towel around it. It is important they be able to move away from the warmth should they wish to so ensure it is tucked in to a corner of their bed with plenty of space. Just as they would go to their mother for warmth, this can act as a replacement.

When it comes to litter box training this again is usually learned from the mother cat as kittens tend to copy her and she will carry them to the tray herself. However, if you are without a mother cat you may have to train your kitten yourself. For young kittens the litter tray needs to be fairly shallow and with soft litter to avoid irritation. After your kitten has eaten move them over to the litter tray and put them in it. You will need to observe them and whenever they display signs of getting ready to excrete move them straight over to the tray. Ensure the tray is situated away from their food and each kitten has their own tray or at least that the try is plenty big enough for the whole litter to be in it at one time; this is in case one kitten or cat guards a tray forcing a timid kitten to go elsewhere.

Watching kittens grow can be a delight for any cat owner and one which brings it's own challenges everyday. However, as long as they are well nourished and have plenty of love and space to grow you will find their development is fast and rewarding.

Chapter 18: When your Scottish Fold Cat Gets Older

1. What can I expect as my cat gets older?

Although cats can now live up to 20 years old cats that are over the age of 10 are generally considered old cats. Scottish Folds have an average life expectancy of around 156 unless they suffer from any of the genetic diseases common with the breed. Indoor cats live much longer than outdoor cats; this is because they have not been exposed to as many infectious diseases, dangerous poisons and fights with other cats, not to mention the perils of crossing roads.

Generally speaking older cats are less active and less inclined to want playtime. They become less sociable and less likely to want stroking, it is important you respect this and do not force them to do anything they do not want to do as they may become aggressive. The need for a quiet space becomes even more important the older they get and new additions to the house need to be considered carefully; younger and more active pets may not be welcomed.

2. What should I look out for in older cats?

Cats tend to not show signs of weakness so when they are visibly suffering it is important that you take them to the vet first and foremost. Common diseases associated with old age in cats are an overactive thyroid, diabetes, kidney disease, cancer and senility. Although we will outline some of the signs that could point to something being wrong with your cat, no one knows your cat better than you, the owner. If you feel something is not right there is no better way to find out for sure than to take your cat to the veterinary clinic and seek some professional advice where they can effectively examine your cat.

As cats age arthritis can be a common problem, this displays itself through your cat becoming much les agile and less willing to jump to large heights as they would do when they were younger. They may also become slightly less naturally groomed as they struggle to clean themselves as adequately as before, but these are subtle changes.

Signs of kidney disease can be difficult to detect but overall you should notice they drink more and urinate more frequently than usual. These again, are subtle changes but if detected early vets can do a lot to stave off the symptoms of chronic kidney disease. There is no cure but in addition to veterinary supplied drugs you can reduce the levels of protein and phosphorus in their diet. The most effective way to do this is to make the dinners yourself and get a diet prescribed by your veterinarian.

Dental problems are one of the most costly consequences of an aging cat. This is an especially damaging problem as it is ultimately very painful for your cat and if left untreated could develop in to an abscess. If you ever feel like your cat's breath is foul, don't assume that it is natural. This is a definite indicator of bad oral health. If you notice bad breath and drooling, there are chances that your cat has tooth decay or gum diseases. Get your cat's teeth checked annually and your vet will be able to provide you with dental services for your cat if they are needed. If there are any evident signs of oral issues, make sure you give your vet details and never ignore even the slightest detail like bleeding of the gums after food, drooling and bad breath. Unfortunately, the most effective prevention is brushing your cat's teeth, but the chances of having a cat that will endure such torture is very rare, however we can offer some advice if you wish to attempt it.

You can start by cleaning your cat's teeth with gauze or cotton before actually proceeding to a brush. To start with, you can just dip your finger in some tuna water and rub it along her teeth and gums to make sure she is conditioned to enjoy the brushing routines. When you begin to brush your cat's teeth, make sure you use specially created cat toothpaste.

Occasionally you could massage her gums; in the case of existing gum problems, massaging will help speed up the healing process. The gums of your cat also become stronger if you do this. The ideal color for your cat's gums is pink. If they are reddish, then this is a sign of infection and irritation.

When your cat reaches 10 years old start introducing enzymatic chews to them to help stave off plaque. However, dental cleaning is the most surefire way to prevent any serious problems and this needs to be done under anesthetic at your veterinary clinic.

Again, it is important to reiterate that you should make sure your cat's dental health routine is regular and must never wait until the last minute. Dental procedures are extremely expensive and are also highly stressful for the cat.

Weight loss can be common with older cats too. This is due to a combination of their senses becoming less potent and a decreased level of activity. To help keep an older cat well-nourished try giving them frequent but smaller meals. As they get older they may become a little fussier, cats are obviously creatures of habit and you will find that changing their food will become near impossible. If you think they are having trouble eating the food you could try warming their meals, this will soften them up and hopefully make them a little more appetizing for them. As with a cat of any age it is vital they keep eating a good proportion of wet food to keep their water levels up.

However, although weight loss is a problem that should be avoided, weight gain is a more prevalent issue. To see the issues that arise from overweight cats please refer to Chapter 14.

Overall, older cats can be just as cute and entertaining as when they were younger. They just like to be kept happy, healthy and relaxed.

Conclusion

So, as you may have gathered, the decision to own a Scottish Fold cat is a complex and considered one to make. It would seem that the controversy surrounding the breeding is definitely warranted. What you need to ask yourself is the following questions:

- Am I so attached the 'folded ears' of the Scottish Fold?
- Do I want the folded ears above a healthy cat?
- Am I willing to pay for the necessary procedures if I have a folded ear cat?
- Do I value the Scottish Fold's other attributes above that of the folded ears?

These are very important questions to consider and your answer does not necessarily dictate whether you buy a Scottish Fold or not. It simply dictates which type you buy. Scottish Folds without the folded ears are much less likely to have the medical problems and as long as they are spayed/neutered, pose little threat to passing on the folded gene.

However despite all the fuss regarding their genetics it is important to realize that these cats are still popular and as much as their very existence offends many cat fanciers, it is still important that owners know how to look after them. Most importantly, you need to look out for the health problems and see that they are handled as quickly and non-invasively as possible. It seems the breed is well equipped to deal with stressful situations and that's just as good, as you may find yourself becoming very familiar with your veterinary clinic. Of course, we are erring on the side of caution here and there is every possibility your Scottish Fold will live a normal healthy life. I just hope we have provided you with all the information you need, just in case.

Other than the possibility of medical complications, Scottish Folds are not just popular because of their distinctive appearance.

It is their loving nature and relaxed temperament which has garnered the most praise.

The Scottish Fold is a wonderful cat, a great companion and truly one of the most loyal cat breeds around. It is rare you hear of one who is naughty, and even rarer to hear them meow! Scottish Fold owners sing their praises whenever they are given the chance and you will find yourself joining in the chorus.

Published by IMB Publishing 2014

Lightning Source UK Ltd.
Milton Keynes UK
UKHW020650180121
377244UK00011B/1112